What people (might) say about Uncivilized (had I actually asked them):

"This is unquestionably the greatest book I have ever read. Chad is brilliant. If his brother were to write a book, I am sure it would be equally as good."

— Chad's mother

"I read it. It doesn't suck."

— Chad's friend Brent

"Please buy this book. In fact buy several copies and hand them out. I don't want to have to deal with a garage full of these things."

— Chad's wife

"Chad who? No I am not going to write a blurb for the front of his book. Now, someone pass me the Gringo Killer Salsa."

— David Crowder

UNCiVILIZED

Pursuing a Shameless Faith

CHAD GOODWILL

UNCiVILIZED
Published by Fusion Press
8172 Contingo Terrace
Kalamazoo, MI 49009

The movies, music and various other vestiges of popular culture referenced throughout this book are offered as anecdotal segues to whatever point the author happens to be trying to make at the time. They are not intended as an endorsement on the part of Fusion Press. On the other hand we vigerously endorse Bilbo's Pizza in a Pan, English Premier League soccer, the color orange, and father/daughter dances.

Unless otherwise identified, all Scripture references are taken from the Holy Bible, New International Version ®. NIV® . Copyright © 1973, 1978, 1984 by International Bible Society. Used by permission of Zondervan. All rights reserved.

ISBN 978-0-615-38791-8

Goodwill, Chad
        Uncivilized: Pursuing a Shameless Faith / Chad Goodwill
1. Authentic life. 2. Christian Living.

Cover Design: Mary Haskin, Scott Millen and the team at Pivotal Communications
Author Photo: Scott Millen

Printed in the United States of America
First Edition 2010

We have no idea why it is so important that we include this series of numbers, but every book we see appears to have them. So we have included them. Please enjoy.

1 2 3 4 5 6 7 8 9 10 / 10 09 08 07 06

Saute diced onion, green pepper and garlic cloves in olive oil. Add diced fresh tomatoes, tomatoe sauce, fresh basil, crushed red pepper, and a little sugar. Let simmer.
Serve over pasta.

To my wife.
I am hopelessly, recklessly, passionately in love with you.

Table of Contents

Acknowledgements

It says in Ecclesiastes that there is nothing new under the sun. In the spirit of that statement, I confess that this book has been heavily influenced by all of the books, sermons, podcasts, and various other forms of communication to which I have been exposed over the years. I don't know that there is any shockingly profound original thought, as much as there is a new way to combine these thoughts such that it provokes a change in your life. That being the case, I am indebted to all of the authors, pastors and friends who were bold enough to speak into my life through their preferred media.

I am grateful to my proofreading team. These people put tremendous effort into making this a better book. Kennedy Filler, Erin Gregorski, Brent Kerstetter, Justin Machnik, and Patrizia Machnik.

A special thanks needs to go out to my friends and family who encouraged me to even start this project. They were so supportive and helped me to see the value in the effort, especially Pat VanderBush and Marty Breithaupt.

I am grateful to my mom and dad for raising me up in the way I should go. I am now able to build on the strong foundation they laid.

I want to thank my brother Scott for making sure that this was hermeneutically sound. And also for laughing at all of my jokes and not holding everything that I did to him while we were growing up against me. Scott has been so consistently there for me and has cared about me enough to be willing to say hard things to me because he knows I need to hear them. I am a better person for having him as my brother. I've got your back too.

If it were not for my wife, Jennifer, this book would have never been printed. Her ceaseless encouragement, optimism and support were vital to completing this project. Even when I ran something by her for the tenth time, she gave me her full attention and invaluable insight. Thank you love.

x

Forward

Safe is comfortable. Safe is warm and cozy and familiar. Safe is vanilla, a navy suit, and fitting in. But nothing monumental or wonderful comes from safe. A runner is safe on base, but he cannot score by staying on base. A ship is safe at harbor, but ships are not made to sit in a harbor. A violin is safe in its case, but what good is that really? Likewise we are all safe when we look like everyone else or act like everyone else or don't do much to challenge others or let on that we may espouse a different world view. But that is not how we were made. Being safe is not how we are meant to behave. To paraphrase a popular bumper sticker:

*Well behaved people
seldom make history.*

We are called to reckless abandon. We are called to push the envelope, test our faith and the faith of others, give up all that would hold us back and vigorously thrash our way through this life so that we create a wake behind us that glorifies God. My hope is that this book will serve to provide either the framework or the kick in the pants people need to embrace a reckless abandon.

That being the case, this book may not be for everyone. If you are content with a trivial existence where you are neither salt nor light, where passion, conviction and pressure are regrettable inconveniences, then put this back on the shelf. Go find a book that will placate you by telling you how God loves you just the way you are and there is no need for you to change. If, however, you are consistently aware of a general uneasiness about you; if your legs twitch because they are desperate to run; if you feel that sometimes it's all that you can do to not scream out at the top of your lungs, then sit down and buckle up. Because as David Crowder says:

*All right.
We are fixin' to get a little bit
uncivilized.*

I figured that it might help if I sort of let you in on the overall map of this book before we get started. That way, there won't be any surprise bends in the road for you. This book is made up of four sections:

- The What
- The How
- The Why
- The Challenge

The What is the section that defines exactly what it is that we are talking about and lay out our objective. What does it mean to be Uncivilized? How is that different from what we see going on around us? We will address how we should behave, what our life should look like, and so on. This section states the case that we need to subscribe to a different perspective. There is a need to be uncivilized and hold to a greater cause.

The How discusses the more practical issues of how we do this. How do we be the way we were made? What specific changes can we make to ensure this will be a real change that will last in our lives? We will discuss being authentic, being childlike and the relationships we need to have in our lives that will help us make the important changes that need to be made. It will provide us with the tools we need to build a life of significance.

The Why answers the question: So what, right? Let's say that all of this uncivilized stuff is true. Why should you care? Why bother putting yourself through all of this anyway? This section details our motivation for living an uncivilized life. Looking beyond the self-help/self-improvement issues, we will learn why a commitment to being uncivilized is so important.

The Challenge explains that this is not all downhill. Once you make the decision to commit to an uncivilized life, the sky doesn't suddenly turn blue and the traffic clear. It's going to be a journey, a battle, a challenge. This section of the book lays this out and discusses what the challenges may be and how we deal with them to stay on course.

Throughout the book, we are going find out who we really are on the inside. What are we like when no one else is around? Why is it we behave the way we do? We have all these things we do because of what people expect from us and the image we are trying to present. We will take a good look at ourselves, find out the things we are passionate about, the things we are excited about, and make those the priorities. We will take the curtain away from real emotions. Because when we leave the curtain covering our emotions, we take away the extent to which we experience life. We have zeal and exuberance that we temper, and they are aching to be set free. We may feel like dancing and shouting, but by the time our behavior goes through all of our processing, we just nod our head and smile. We need to get back to the point where we actually dance and shout and sing.

Once we have established who we really are, we will discover that the most important thing is we need to be the person that God has called us to be. Who is it that God says that we are? If for no other reason, we need to pursue this out of the obligation that God is GOD. He is the King of the Universe, Master of everything. God encourages us to be like a child, but what does that mean? How do we go about accomplishing this on a daily basis? Then we will hit the ground running. We will have the understanding, the tools, and know what to expect when we are brave enough to live out loud.

In order to maintain gender neutrality in the book. I made the decision to apply gender-specific pronouns on an every-other-chapter basis (he/she; him/her, etc.). So the even number chapters are woman-specific and the men get the odd ones. Don't read anything into that.

Here we go.

The What

Chapter 1

Feels like I'm tied up. What's holding me?
I want to live like there's no tomorrow.
I want to dance like no one's around.
I want to sing like nobody's listening, as I lay my
body down.
I want to give like I have plenty.
I want to love like I'm not afraid.
I want to be the man I was meant to be.
I want to be the way I was made.

The Way I was Made — Ed Cash, Jesse Reeves
and Chris Tomlin[1]

Be Uncivilized

I love those lyrics. I remember the first time I heard this song. I thought wouldn't that be great if someone could really do that? How liberating would it be to live a life where you knew exactly how you were made and you lived that out in such a way that other people's opinions of you provided no material influence to your behavior? I was chewing on that thought for a while and finally came to the realization that these lyrics were not describing some whimsical Utopia, but were a call to action. We need to be the way we were made. But how exactly are we made?

One of my favorite things to do in Chicago is to go to the Art Institute and look at the painting called A Sunday on La Grande Jatte by George Seurat. It's amazing to think that this huge brilliant work of art is nothing more than a collection of dots (pointillism). An interesting thing about his method is that instead of using a specific colored dot, like pink, he would place the appropriate colored dots next to each other, like white and red, to cause the eye to see pink.

God has created a canvas as well and we are the dots of paint on that canvas. God has made you in a very specific way. He has given you strengths, characteristics, quirks, and passions that are uniquely yours. He made you to shine a very specific color to the rest of the world. And when we each embrace that which is unique about us and we interact with others who are as genuine as we are, then we combine all of these different colors to create an amazing experience. The canvas ends up being vibrant and beautiful, just as God intended. However, if everyone tries to be like everyone else, then we end up with a boring canvas that is generally just shades of beige, or at best a Jackson Pollack, whose style of painting some would say is similar to what you would expect a drop cloth to look like.

At a certain level, it's acceptable, even appropriate to have various natural demeanors, which will reveal themselves in different environments. Our dress and behavior will be considerably different at a baseball game than it would at church, or at work. This is simply social etiquette. The problem arises when our behavior at that very same baseball game varies depending on the company we keep. Instead of risking revealing our true self, we present ourselves as the person that we feel will impress others. Many people act in the way that they feel the other person expects, and therefore few are truly authentic.

We are not meant to fit in. God did not design us to seamlessly integrate ourselves into the culture at large. We need to take the color that we are made to be and shine that color as bright and strong as we can. We are not to allow our actions to be determined by the influence of others. We are supposed to be … uncivilized.

Uncivilized?!?!

It's OK. Take a deep breath. I did not write some book that is trying to orchestrate the degeneration of dignified behavior. Nor am I trying to convince people to lower the bar. I am simply saying that maybe we need to consider that there is a different bar altogether that we are supposed to be using. So, at the risk of interfering with the picture you have in your head of a Monty Python sketch[2] or a recent report on some teen actress's weekend exploits, I thought I would tell you exactly what I mean by uncivilized.

A civilized person is someone who subscribes to the opinion of society at large regarding what is appropriate behavior. They base their actions on how others will perceive them. They behave in the way that they feel will make others think highly of them. This could mean different things to a lot of people. Maybe it's needing to wear the right clothes or drive the right car. Maybe it's suppressing your emotions in such a way that you do not fully express yourself. Maybe you have a job because it provides the right paycheck, as opposed to feeding your passion. It could be that you listen to specific music, read specific books, or watch specific shows, but not because you are actually interested in any of them yourself. You do it because you want to be popular and be part of the conversations of your peers. I even know of grown adults who have gone so far as listening to Brittany Spears. (I know. Crazy, right?) A civilized person is primarily concerned with fitting in. He plays by the rules. He is normal, common and ordinary.

Therefore, if you are an uncivilized person, you are not primarily concerned with those things. Our first thought is not about fitting in or staying inside the box. Certainly, we do not seek to offend, but we are going to base our actions on the words of the song at the beginning of this chapter. We will be the way we were made. If that is in line with, or in opposition to, what appears to be the flavor of the day, we don't care. We know who we are, and we are going to live our lives accordingly. We are authentic.

We have defined exactly what it is that makes us who we are. We can then take that definition and use it as the basis for determining our actions. We know that we have a purpose in life that cannot be accomplished if we dilute ourselves.

Let's make the argument to be uncivilized a little more practical. I will be the first to admit that civilized behavior is relative. Different periods in history have offered different definitions as to what is civilized. What was considered to be uncivilized at one point in time may be commonplace and entirely acceptable at another time. For example, consider the following list of behavior that was regarded as being socially unacceptable at one point:

- Holding hands in public
- Women wearing pants
- Men not wearing a hat
- Showing a married couple sleeping in the same bed on TV

While these are amusing to us, there is another list that is less amusing. The following is a list of behavior that is now considered to be socially acceptable and even civilized by our culture today:

- Divorce
- Sex outside of marriage
- Lying
- Greed
- Excessive drinking
- Lust
- Selfishness
- Arrogance
- Polka music

I could certainly go on, but I imagine you understand the general direction in which the list would continue. Why do we pattern our lives after what we see on television, or read in magazines, or see others do? Why do we work so hard to "fit in" to the cultural norm when, as we have established, the norm can be pretty pathetic?

Lives That Glorify God

You can call it whatever you want, uncivilized, undignified, unashamed or authentic, but I want to live a life where I forsake my pride and other's opinions of me to live in a way that glorifies God. You see, when our behavior is determined to any extent by our desire to fit in with others, then what we are doing is deferring our will to theirs. We are saying that our worth is no more or no less than what others determine it to be. But you know that is not true. Our worth is determined by God and Him alone.

Yes you should defer your will. But your will should be deferred to God. We will discuss the fear of God in greater detail in a later chapter, but for now, let's acknowledge that our actions are shaped by what we fear. So fear God. Be an authentic person because God has commanded us to and He is God.

As Christ followers, one of the scariest places we can be is in a position where we fit in with the world around us — where we look like and act like everyone else. That cannot be our goal. We don't want to fit in with people who are not going where we are going. Certainly, we want to be with them and interact with them regularly. But when people look at us, they need to see the reflection of God in us. Ephesians 5:1–2 tells us to be imitators of God.

> *Be imitators of God, therefore as dearly loved children and live a life of love, just as Christ loved us and gave himself up for us as a fragrant offering and sacrifice to God.*

A big part of being true to yourself is being true to the way God made you. He made us to be a reflection of Him. Let me give you a great example of someone who understood how he was made and how his behavior was consistent with God's expectations for his life.

There is a passage in the book of 2 Samuel about David. God had given David and his army victory over the Philistines and David was brining the Ark of the Covenant back to Jerusalem. This was a big deal. The Ark was the presence of the Lord and David was finally bringing the presence of the Lord back to Jerusalem. This passage talks about how as the Ark entered Jerusalem, David danced before the Lord with ALL HIS MIGHT. Imagine how enthusiastic and energetic it would look like to dance with all your might. To dance holding nothing back. What a great picture. As David was dancing vigorously, he was inhibited by the robes he wore as king. So he took them off and was dancing in a linen ephod, which was a close-fitting sleeveless undergarment of sorts. That way he could move freely to worship God the way he wanted to given the amazing circumstances. While this was going on, his wife Michal looked through the palace window and saw David dancing through the streets of Jerusalem in his underwear and was ashamed. Michal told David that she thought it was ridiculous for the King of Israel to behave that way in front of everyone. She felt that he was behaving as someone who was uncivilized and shameless. David's response to her was brilliant. Essentially, he said:

> *I behave the way I behave for the Lord and for no one else. If you think that was bad, I will be even more undignified than this because I understand that it is not about me or what people think about me. It is about being humble in my own eyes and serving God the way He wants to be served.*

Isn't that great? That is it. That is what it's all about. Let the way you behave be governed by the Lord and no one else. Forget about what people think or their opinion about you. Be who you were made to be. Do not try to fit in, or keep up, or follow trends.

Who Holds the Standard?

In 1 Corinthians 3:18–19, it says:

> *Do not deceive yourselves. If any one of you thinks he is wise by the standards of this age, he should become a "fool" so that he may become wise. For the wisdom of this world is foolishness in God's sight.*

That is pretty straight forward isn't it? Our behavior needs to be different from what is considered to be wise by the population at large. We need to be set apart. We need to live a life that stands out so much from the crowd that people feel compelled to come up to us and find out what is different about us.

The Bible says in 1 Corinthians 1:19–25:

> *For it is written: "I will destroy the wisdom of the wise; the intelligence*

*of the intelligent I will frustrate."
Where is the wise man? Where is
the scholar? Where is the
philosopher of this age? Has not God
made foolish the wisdom of the
world? For since in the wisdom of
God the world through its wisdom did
not know him, God was pleased
through the foolishness of what was
preached to save those who believe.*

*Jews demand miraculous signs and
Greeks look for wisdom, but we
preach Christ crucified: a stumbling
block to Jews and foolishness to
Gentiles, but to those whom God has
called, both Jews and Greeks, Christ
the power of God and the wisdom of
God. For the foolishness of God is
wiser than man's wisdom, and the
weakness of God is stronger than
man's strength.*

This passage lays out the fact that there is a huge chasm between what we believe to be wise or strong and what God considers to be wise or strong. From where I stand, I may regard six-pack abs or a collection of degrees hanging on the wall as preferable, but God may be trying to tell me that moderation and meekness is what I really need. It's kind of like my six year old daughter coming up to me and "teaching" me the best way to kick a soccer ball. She thinks that she is imparting vast wisdom to me. But compared to what I have to offer, it's kind of silly. So it's in our best interest to not rely on our wisdom. Unless of course your objective is a shallow, empty, frustrating life filled with disappointment and regret. (Not that I am prone to exaggeration.) If so, then "good on ya" and have at it. If not, keep reading and we will discover how to be an authentic person that will be a source of light to people around us.

The Benefit of Living an Authentic Life

When we embrace an uncivilized lifestyle, there are three amazing opportunities that open up for us.

1. We are able to provide real help and support to others.
2. We develop meaningful relationships.
3. We become salt and light.

Support—

Let's say you are driving down the highway and you are starving. You want to find a place to eat that is right off the highway. You don't want to get stuck at one of those exits where they have a sign for food, but when you take the exit, you see that you have to go five miles down the road to get to it. So you keep driving until you see those golden arches on a pole sticking up fifty feet in the air. Then you know that food is right there and easily accessible. There may have actually been a great restaurant that was easily accessible at an earlier exit, but it made no effort to differentiate itself from the horizon. When we are uncivilized, our lives become a beacon for others, like the sign on that fifty foot pole.

We are living in a difficult time right now. We are living through the worst economy since the Great Depression. Unemployment and confidence levels are worse than most of us have ever seen. People are hurting. I am hurting. So let me ask you a question. How can a person in need find their answers in God if the behavior of Christians is such that there is no difference between us and everyone else, if they can't see us sticking up on the horizon? As Christ followers, we have the answers. We hold the cookie. Therefore, our lives need to be lived in such a way as to differentiate us from the people who don't have the answers that hurting people need. Our behavior needs to be striking, an aberration, or even odd as far as that goes. They need to see something in us that they don't see elsewhere.

We become like a breath of fresh air to them. A pleasant surprise from how they expect to see people behave. When they observe freedom in us and see our lives demonstrating the joy and contentment that they seek, then we will have immediate credibility in their eyes. We will be given the opportunity to provide them with the answers that they need — answers that offer them true help and true support.

The great thing about uncivilized behavior is that it is not just about our ability to help others. Making a commitment to being true to who you are also creates an environment where we can receive help. I am sure that you have heard the story of the man whose house was in the middle of a terrible flood. He made it to his roof and was praying for God to save him when someone came by in a raft. He refused help stating that God would keep him safe. A little while later after the water had risen more, a man rowed by in a canoe offering assistance. Again the man refused saying that God would protect him. Finally when the water had risen above the roof line, a helicopter came and the man waived him away with the same sentiment. Well, the man eventually drowned. When he got to heaven, he asked God why He did not keep him safe. God's reply was "I sent a raft, a canoe and a helicopter. What more did you want?"

Someone may have a raft that will help us out of a bad situation. They may have some experience in dealing with a problem with which we are currently struggling. If we are honest about our situation, we will reveal our need and they will be able to offer their raft to us. We will avail ourselves to assistance rather than continue to drown in our circumstances.

Meaningful Relationships—

The irony of working so hard to change who you are to fit in with the right crowd is that when you do eventually fit in with them, you are surrounded by people with whom you have nothing in common. If all that we ever show the world is a thin veneer of a perfect life, we will simply gloss over anything of substance with each other. But, uncivilized people have gone through the process of defining who they are. They then live that out, which leads to authentic relationships with like-minded people who are going the same way they are.

Salt and Light—

Matthew 5:13–16 says:

> *You are the salt of the earth. But if the salt loses its saltiness, how can it be made salty again? It is no longer good for anything, except to be thrown out and trampled by men.*
>
> *You are the light of the world. A city on a hill cannot be hidden. Neither do people light a lamp and put it under a bowl. Instead they put it on its stand, and it gives light to everyone in the house. In the same way, let your light shine before men, that they may see your good deeds and praise your Father in heaven.*

Be Uncivilized

Salt preserves and light illuminates. As a Christ follower, it's your life that God will use to advance His kingdom on Earth. As such, we need to make sure that our lives are effective for that purpose. If you let your life fully reflect God and live the way that He designed you to live, you will be salt and light to everyone around you. This is a life that glorifies God. If we just fit in, how will others ever be drawn to the light of God in us? We have to live a life that others will find remarkable and that will cause others to want what we have. We cannot be the same stale status quo that they experience from everyone else.

Who Am I to Talk?

I remember learning at an early age to pay attention to what people choose to criticize in others, because you will find that that is the very issue with which they struggle. Just as an honest man presumes others to be honest, a greedy man will suspect others of being greedy. I am being critical of this issue because, well, I am the chief of sinners. I am able to write about being uncivilized because I have struggled with it, and probably will at some level for the rest of my life. I have found myself playing these games, or wearing these masks, much to my detriment.

I have, throughout my life, become increasingly aware of both how our insecurity evidences itself through the masks we wear and the necessity for honesty in our relationships. We start out all right until we learn that honesty and popularity are not necessarily bedfellows. We tell ourselves that we don't lie per se, but we may enhance the truth, just enough to make ourselves look good. Then we win the prize. It's hard to beat that immediate gratification from stretching the truth about who we really are. The problem is that there is the TRUTH, and it's an absolute. There are not varying degrees of truth. There is not a relative truth. When it comes right down to it there is the truth and anything else has a mouth full of Dial soap at the end of it. And why Dial anyway? That was the vilest tasting stuff. Kids today have it off easy. They get this herbal, fruity, glycerin frou-frou stuff. No wonder kids lie more today...but I digress.

I used to be in corporate banking. In that industry there are some people who are concerned about projecting the right image and posturing to impress others. They have to wear the right suits and shoes, drive the right car, have the right acquaintances... (Are you sensing a trend?) I went back to school and earned an MBA in finance, not because it had any real direct applicable skill set that would contribute to my job. I did it because it's what corporate bankers do. How stupid is that? You eventually wake up one day and realize that you are simply playing games. That is when you

13

throw the lace-up cap toe shoes to the back of the closet and grab your Birkenstocks and head to the office. (Which HR quickly informed me was not acceptable according to the dress code, so I had to go home and change.)

We do all this posturing to imply that we have arrived, but no one has "arrived". No one has it all together. We are all on a constant journey of learning and improving ourselves. Life is too short to believe otherwise. When we are young, we feel invincible, like we will live forever. However, as we get older, we are increasingly shocked at how quickly the years go by. My hope is that everyone would be blessed with the perspective of our parents or grandparents while we are still young. To have the ability to see what is truly important before we waste our lives chasing the wrong things would be priceless.

My grandpa Monson was so cool. He did not give a hoot about what people thought of him. We would pick him up for church and he would have on green plaid pants, a brown plaid jacket and a blue tie. My mom would laugh and tell him that he could not go out like that. He would just huff and say "Carol, I don't care." He knew who he was and no one else's opinion was going to change that.

It's not worth the time and energy to be anything other than the way God made us to be. We need to constantly be aware of how vain and futile it is to attempt to present some alternate image of ourselves to others. I hope that you are able to take a close look at why you do the things that you do. I hope that you will be challenged to reconsider preconceptions that you have and will risk being real. Risk being the way you were made. So let's do it. Let's throw caution to the wind, rally the troops, sound the alarm. Let's live an uncivilized life.

Chapter 2

I'm not sure what I'm looking for anymore
I just know that I'm harder to console
I don't see who I'm trying to be instead of me
But the key is a question of control

All this running around, well it's getting me down
Just give me a pain that I'm used to
I don't need to believe all the dreams you
conceive
You just need to achieve something that rings
true

A Pain That I am Used To— Depeche Mode[3]

Know Thyself

I like pencils. I like the tactile sensation of the carbon scraping across the page. I like the feeling of a fresh start every time you begin to write after pulling one out of the sharpener. There is a sense of accomplishment when you have worn it down to the point where you can't really write with it anymore and you take a new one out of the box. Pencils are old school, not flashy or trendy or pretentious. You don't hear people boasting about owning a $300 pencil. They don't come with lights or in unorthodox shapes. They don't sing to you when you write with them. They are classic.

We are designed to more closely approximate a pencil. We are designed to understand exactly who we are, how we are made, and what our purpose is. We are to maintain our focus on those things and not get preoccupied by all that tries to distract us to become something else. I find that others are drawn to people whose lives reflect that commitment to authenticity similar to the way you are drawn to the familiar smell and feel of a freshly sharpened pencil.

I have a friend with whom I was discussing the topic of being an uncivilized person. He confided in me with a comment that I am sure is not particular to him. He said that he has lived his life trying to please other people for so long, that he does not know who he is at this point. My friend's entire identity has become wrapped up acting the way that he thinks others want him to.

This friend's circumstance is described by the lyrics at the beginning of this chapter: I can't see who I am trying to be anymore; there is a hole in me and I am desperate to have something that is real. That song, *A Pain That I'm Used To*, is by the group Depeche Mode. They do not subscribe to the Christian world view, but you can hear the longing in the lyrics for something real, something of substance. They are longing for a hint of something genuine because they no longer know who they are or what they are chasing.

So at this point, I want to ask you: Who are you? If you strip all of the noise and static away, what are you really like on the inside? Defining who you are is the first step toward authenticity. For many people, this will be an easy and fun question to answer. But for others, like my friend, this may be painfully revealing.

To start, let's agree that our behavior is currently influenced by outside sources to a greater degree than we like, or even know. In this

17

chapter, we will work through these influences so that we understand them well enough to set them aside for our journey of self discovery.[4]

Outside Influence

David Wells wrote a great book titled: *No Place for Truth, or Whatever Happened to Evangelical Theology.* (I love that title because it reminds me of the Rocky and Bullwinkle cartoons I watched when I was a kid— yes I am showing my age here— where they would display a shot of Boris Badenov twisting his mustache and the announcer would say: "Tune in next week for The Incredible Train Wreck, or Can Moose Really Fly?") In his book, he talks about a World Cliché Culture and about how we are all others-centered. By this he is talking about how we center our lives around the influences of others. He proposes that we are attuned to experiences and appearances, not to thought or character. "What shapes the modern world is not powerful minds but powerful forces, not philosophy but urbanization, capitalism, and technology. As the older quest for truth has collapsed, intellectual life has increasingly become little more than a gloss on the processes of modernization."[5]

Because we are living in a world where so many people consider most things to be relative, there is a glaring lack of people who hold to an absolute truth. And those who do, find it very difficult to assert their beliefs because of the harassment they receive from others. But does that mean that we should abandon ourselves to this culture?

Society appears to be evolving into two separate worlds. First, we have the world of who we authentically are. This is essentially our true self, the way we behave around our family and friends. Secondly, we have the outside world. This is the world where we are only recognized for what we do. In this outside world, authenticity may prove detrimental. We are often rewarded for our ability to be impersonal. Unfortunately, this outside oriented world seems to be growing in prevalence.

For example, one of the hardest things that I ever had to do as a banker was to execute an exit strategy for an existing client. This is where we ask a client to find financing elsewhere for a variety of reasons. In this situation, I am encouraged to be "strictly business" and just represent the bank. This exactly represents the outside perspective. But the truth is that there are occasions where this is painful to the client, and I feel bad for them. I do all that I can to help them through the situation, I encourage them, and in as much as is reasonable, I demonstrate love to them. In each case, they have responded well to my genuine concern for them. If I had just been an impersonal banker, circumstances would have worked themselves out differently. By "differently", I mean poorly.

I find it striking that we all seem to hold the view that WE are the normal people, but everyone else is a part of the impersonal culture we just discussed. Coincidentally, the person next to you feels that THEY are the normal one and you are just part of that callous world. We all want the personal world to take over the outside world. It's just that no one wants to take the first step. So we all just numb ourselves with a watered down friendliness due to the demands of propriety.

Others Centered

We have become others-centered. Our closets are full of clothes we bought because we want to be cool. I mean, come on, who would honestly ever wear high-heeled shoes or a suit and tie on a 95 degree day if left to themselves? We watch movies, watch TV, read magazines, follow celebrities and essentially defer to all of the influences around us. As Christ followers, we should be concerned. We should be very concerned.

Sociologists recently conducted a low profile survey on Hollywood's elite. One hundred and four of the most influential television writers and producers were asked a host of ideological questions. Considering what we see coming out of Hollywood, the findings are quite predictable:

- 93 percent seldom or never attend worship services
- 97 percent believe in a woman's right to abort
- 16 percent strongly agree that adultery is wrong
- 99 percent believe that television should be more critical of Judeo-Christian values[6]

So why do we do this? Why do we let the influence of people with this type of orientation change our behavior? There are two primary motives that would cause us to choose to present an image of ourselves that is different from who we really are. We are either masking an insecurity that cripples us into thinking that we are only as good as other people think we are. Or we are grasping for something in greed or selfish ambition.

Everyone has some insecurity. If someone tells you otherwise, they are lying to you because they are insecure and are afraid that you will think less of them. The truth is that you will never be good enough. The world will never let you be good enough, good looking enough, rich enough, physically fit enough, or successful enough. You will always be left wanting more, feeling like you have more to prove. You are always going to feel like you need one more thing: if you only made a little more money, if you only had a different spouse, a better job, a bigger house, or hair (but that one may only apply to me), etc. Essentially what you are doing is allowing the things you are chasing to define you, as opposed to having a solid definition of who you are before you even walk out the door.

We let ourselves become subject to an external determination of what it means to be successful, popular, or refined. The inference being that someone who is refined is a better person or more important than someone who is not. And all of this alleviates our insecurities. But is that what is going to make you more likable? If you ask most people whom they would rather befriend, it will be the person who is real, who is approachable, loving, trustworthy, what you see is what you get. As opposed to someone who puts on airs, or acts with pretense, or speaks out of both sides of their mouth. A preschool teacher versus a politician.

Deep inside, we think that we are not worthy. We are not what people think we are. Behind closed doors, we are weak, insecure, dumb, or unattractive. For some people, this may be something very slight. For others, it may be quite glaring. We have things that we do not want people to know, so we behave in a manner that will lead people to believe something other than that about us. We alter our natural behavior because we want people to think a certain way about us. But if you do that and you convince people that you are someone that you are not, you end up in a group or an area that is unfamiliar to you. The way that you are behaving in order to garner other people's affection is not who you really are. Conducting oneself in this fashion then leads to more internal conflict. If you simply behave in a manner consistent with the way you were made, people will respond well to you. You can be honest with people and people can be honest with you. You would have healthier relationships and a healthier lifestyle.

Crossing the Line

Granted, some of our behavior is going to be cultural. For example, some cultures use dance as an everyday part of their celebration. Some cultures express affection more openly than others. Some are more vocal, and so on. So culturally, we are taught that there is a certain way we are to behave. This is great, and healthy. Social etiquette can be a good thing. It's professional for a banker to wear a suit. Suits are good. I would be very much opposed to going to work naked. So the question of the day is: When do we cross the line between etiquette and affectation? In other words, when do we stop being polite and start being something that we are not? Where is this line for each of us? How do we recognize the line and what should our response be when we do?

My point in discussing affected behavior is not to advocate anarchy or a social uprising, as fun as that would be to watch. The point is actually a very subtle difference, and you are the only one who can determine which side of the line you are on. Life is full of lines that we flirt with every day. Some we cross, others we don't. Some lines are obvious, like the centerline of a highway. Others are very difficult to define like the difference between being confident and being arrogant. Often times there is no real harm in crossing a line, but sometimes it can lead to dangerous territory. When your attitude crosses the line from simply being confident of your God-given abilities to being arrogant, you go from being someone that people will rally behind to someone whom people avoid. Likewise when our behavior flirts with the line between that which is social etiquette and that which is affected behavior, it can lead us down a difficult path.

- Do we wear clothes appropriate for the situation, or do we have to wear clothes with the appropriate label?
- Do we have a car to get us around town, or do we have a car to make people look at us?
- Do we listen to music because we enjoy it, or because we enjoy the response we get from our friends?
- Do we have a job that is meaningful to us or a job that we need to support a lifestyle that others will feel is meaningful?
- Do we use a certain vocabulary, express ourselves a certain way, or do anything because it's inherently significant to us or because we want to be perceived as significant?

Do you know what I am saying? A Hummer is a perfect vehicle if you are in the military, or own a large ranch with rough terrain, or are an outfitter and need to get to hard to reach trailheads. But if you are just going to the grocery store and soccer practice, then you have to wonder what your motivation is. You are the only one who can answer these questions. No one can make the determination for you. Everything can be an effective tool. Only the user of the tool will determine if its use is ultimately good or bad. Are all these things we do just masks we wear to present ourselves to the world? There is a word that is used to describe an actor who would don different masks as she acted her parts on the stage. She is called a Hypocrite.

We live in the world, but we do not have to subscribe to everything it has to offer. 1 John 2:15 says:

> *Do not love the world or anything in the world. If anyone loves the world, the love of the Father is not in him. For everything in the world — the cravings of sinful man, the lust of his eyes and the boasting of what he has and does — comes not from the Father but from the world. The world and its desires pass away, but the man who does the will of God lives forever.*

We are in the world, but we are not of the world. A great example of this that I have seen is in the movie The Matrix. In case you are one of the eleven people who have not seen this movie, I will set the scene up for you. There is this guy named Neo. He is the hero, but doesn't know it. So throughout much of the movie, the other characters are working to convince him of the fact that he is the chosen one, and that the world that he sees around him does not exist as he thinks. They are trying to explain that what he sees is simply a computer program.

Neo asks Morpheus (the father figure) "What are you telling me? That I can ... dodge bullets?" And Morpheus replies "No Neo. I am telling you that when you are ready ... you won't have to." (Cue the chill down the spine.) So we get to the end of the movie and there is the big showdown between Neo and the antagonist, Mr. Smith. Neo starts to look around and everything suddenly clicks. The images fade and Neo can finally see everything as ones and zeroes in the computer program. Mr. Smith unloads his entire magazine of bullets at Neo and Neo looks at the bullets curiously, and causes them to stop in mid air and fall harmlessly to the ground. He finally understands what everyone was telling him. Although the world he sees around him seems incredibly real, it does not actually hold anything over him. In truth, he lives outside it.

This is the epiphany that we need to have. Yes we are in the world. Everything around us is very real in a certain way. But, we are not subject to this world. We are like Neo. We are simply passing through and are here to force the world to be subject to a greater truth, rather than having the world force its "truth" on us.

So let's look at the two sides of the equation here that will give us a clearer picture of who we are. First are the bad things in us that need to be diminished and second are the good things in us that need to be accentuated. As we go through this exercise, we will see a much clearer image of how we were made.

The Empire

Now that we have identified that there is a measure of us that we have allowed to be defined by others, let's take a look at the rest of us. Let's look at who we are without regard to outside influence. The problem is, just like in Star Wars, there is a good side (The Rebellion) and a dark side (The Empire) to the force. Right now I want to briefly look at the dark side. So be strong.

We are all sinners. That is not news to anyone. Romans 3:23 says that all have sinned and fallen short of the glory of God. In Mark 10:18, Jesus says that no one is good except God alone. The only good in us is that which has been given to us through the work of the Holy Spirit in our lives. So the introspection I am about to advocate will reveal things about us that will need to change. There is no sense in putting a band aid on a broken leg. I want us to be completely honest with ourselves here. Our goal is to be a better person and to become more Christ-like. As such, we need to not gloss over our deficiencies.

The primary, and most logical, method for discovering deficiencies in our lives is to find the areas in your life that are not consistent with the outline for living that God has provided us. Some people refer to this as the Bible. I could recite a thousand verses that talk about a proper perspective, a right attitude or appropriate actions, but they print these Bibles every day. I figure you could just go out and get one yourself. That will work better anyway because no one likes to be told what to do. So if you read these verses yourselves, you will feel like it's your idea and you will be much more motivated that way. I will risk quoting one verse because it's one of my favorites. The verse is found in Colossians 3:12–14:

> *Therefore, as God's chosen people,*
> *holy and dearly loved, clothe*
> *yourselves with compassion,*
> *kindness, humility, gentleness and*
> *patience. Bear with each other and*
> *forgive whatever grievances you may*
> *have against one another. Forgive as*

*the Lord forgave you. And over all
these virtues, put on love, which
binds them all together in perfect
unity.*

Everyone talks about the great mysteries of the Bible and the struggle for understanding and enlightenment, but this verse is not one of those mysteries. The instruction on the characteristics that should be demonstrated in our life is pretty straightforward. And there are piles of other verses just like this one that are not shrouded in mystery. If the Bible says clothe yourself with gentleness and patience, then be on guard for areas in your life where you are not gentle or patient. I know, this is really deep, complicated, rocket scientist stuff, isn't it?

All kidding aside, we will go through phases in our lives where certain things in the Bible will jump out at us more than others. Next time, before you sit down to read the Bible, pray to have God show you things in His word that you need to incorporate into your life. Behavior that you may currently exhibit that you need to change. And then dive in. God is faithful to lead you to where you need to be.

Another of the more effective ways to see areas in your life that will need to be addressed is to pay close attention to that which tends to upset you when you see it evidenced in others. Another way to word that is: What are the things about which you tend to be critical?

When this question sank in with me, I was able to work out several issues in my life. The first was greed. I was, by nature, a very greedy, self-concerned person. When I saw how upset it made me when I saw those traits in others, a light went off. It was as though a TV appeared in my head and an episode of "This is Your Dysfunction" began to play. I saw how I needed to address these issues in my life. When I finally did, it did not bother me as much when I saw that behavior in others.

We will need to ask this question to ourselves for the rest of our lives. These revelations can show up in strange ways as well. For example, I have been accused of being too driven and working too hard. I did not think much of it because I would rather err on the side of working too hard. Then I started to think about it because I tend to be very hard on what I perceive as laziness in other people. It's one of my primary triggers that makes it difficult for me to respect others. It turns out that I am so afraid of being lazy, that I work inordinately hard to compensate, or should I say over-compensate, for it. So I am working through this right now in my life. I am trying to find a happy medium between being a slacker and being Martha Stewart. (I love Martha Stewart by the way.)

The third method is to take advantage of very close friends, who will speak to you in love, and can help you identify some areas in your life that should change. Identifying our shortcomings is the part that stinks, because it's hard when we take the masks off and do not like what we see behind them. But having an accurate understanding of who we are is so important. There is no point in being authentic if we are by nature authentically obnoxious. I will get into relationships in greater detail in a later chapter, so I won't dwell on them now. But suffice it to say that there are people in your life who love you and want the best for you and are willing to help you along this journey. Use them. Don't let pride interfere. I recently encouraged a buddy of mine to find some people to help him accomplish a goal he has in his life. He told me that he is all about self-control and self-discipline, but he hates to have others tell him what to do. If he does not let go of his aversion to receiving help, he will forfeit a tremendous amount of potential in his life. We can only go so far on our own, and often we are blind to our own shortcomings. God knows I am.

So make your list.
- What are things about which you are critical? What could this be masking?
- What do you know for a fact are areas of your life that do not line up with God's word? I want the big areas here — not symptoms, but root causes.
- What are issues that others see evidenced in your life that need to be addressed?
- What are things about you that would prove to be counterproductive with the salt and light effort? I don't care about the quirkiness that not everyone finds endearing. What do you do that does not show God's love?

This is the first part. The bad that needs to be eliminated.

The Rebellion

Now for the fun part — the good side of the force. Let's find the diamond in the rough here. Each one of us has fantastic qualities that make us different from every other person on earth. If we just embrace these differences and don't mask them in front of others, then together we create something amazing. Getting back to our pointillism analogy, here is where we discover what a brilliant color you are.

I am going to make you work now. I want you to get a pen and some paper and make a list. I want you to take this seriously. Put some thought and effort into this. I want you to make a list of your passions. Come up with at least ten things. If you cannot come up with ten things, then your life is too boring and you need to hang out with me or David Crowder[7] for a while until we get some legs under you.

These passions can be many things: hobbies (cooking, stamp collecting, English Premier League soccer), roles (student, parent, spouse, employee), interests (cycling, reading, playing guitar), attitudes (honesty, compassion, being uncivilized), anything. But you have to be passionate about them, I mean boundless enthusiasm. This is something that you could talk about for an hour at the next cocktail party. Something you would never choose to live life without. So take your time. We are attempting to identify the you that is inside there. Let me go over a few of the items on my list for you so you get an idea of what I am talking about.

Family — I love my family. I adore my family. I would die for my wife and kids. Their happiness and safety takes precedence over any desire that I may have. Because I am sure that you want to know, I have been married to Jennifer for 17 years. I have a 10-year old named Madeline, a 7-year old named Meghan, and a 3-year old named Maille. No I did not intend to name all of them "M" names, it just happened. Actually the first two just happened. My wife was concerned that if we did not name the third an "M" name then she would feel left out. So there you go. See, this fits my definition because I have gone on for about an hour.

Music — Music speaks to my soul. To live a life without music is like watching a black and white TV. You get the picture, but miss all of the passion. I constantly have music around. Many kinds of music depending on the situation. My favorite part about the Ally McBeal show was that I discovered I was not the only person who has theme songs that play in their heads at different times. Music can mark amazing moments in our life in a way that nothing else can.

Worship — I love to worship God. There is no other way that I have found that can give me a sense of how amazing God is. It can be in my car, at home, at church, anywhere. Worship gives me the opportunity to demonstrate to God that He means everything to me, that life is all about Him, and to thank Him for all He has done in my life.

Relationships — We are on earth for two primary reasons. To give God glory and to develop relationships with others. I love to interact with people as deeply as I can. Sometimes it's only for a few minutes as I am checking in to a hotel. Other times these interactions can be stimulating conversation during a fantastic time spent with close friends. Life is not about me. Life is about how I can interact with others to have meaningful relationships. My brother thinks that I am strange because I will go up to anyone at any time and have a conversation, but that is what it's all about, isn't it? I am one color and he is another. (Secretly though, I think he was adopted.)

Some other things that would make my list would be fitness, writing, love, good food, and reading. I want to emphasize again that these have to be things that you feel very strongly about. Things that are a primary part of your life and things that you would never choose to do without. This is not a wish list. Don't put an item down if it's something that you would like to do but have not picked up yet. These are obsessions in your life that push everything else to the side. I am a runner. I love the solitude, exhilaration, pain and fitness that it brings. I plan my runs and work the rest of my schedule around them. That is what I am talking about.

Don't make this task entirely an exercise in introspection. Introspection is good because you are the only one who can hear the voices inside your head. (Although, I would not tell too many people that you hear those voices.) You are the only one who really knows what makes you tick. Having said that, it's a good idea to go to others and ask them their opinion about you. What is it about you that draws them to you? What do they consider your passions to be based on how they see you spend your time or how you respond to them? What do they see in you that makes you unique? Obviously, these people will have to be very close friends or family members. They need to be able to both identify these apparent passions and feel comfortable enough with you to speak into your life in this manner.

Take a deep breath. Defining your passions is a big deal. You are taking a significant step toward defining who you are apart from anything going on outside of you. The list is a tool that will help you to embrace that which makes you distinct. Defining these passions will also help you make difficult decisions when you are being pulled in wrong directions.

Use this list of passions. Embrace it. You do not even have to stop at ten. The list is what defines who you are proactively. For the most part, you can be reasonably confident that God has given you these passions that make you unique. There is a verse in Psalms that, when interpreted properly, makes this point.

Psalm 37:4
*Delight yourself in the Lord and He
will give you the desires of your heart.*

Contrary to what you hear a lot of talking heads say, I do not believe that this means that God will give you whatever you want. I believe David (the author of this Psalm) is saying that God puts the desires and passions in your heart that He wants you to have. He influences us to desire the best things for us.

Let these passions be a tool for you. Memorize them and be confident in them. Put them on your bathroom mirror or inside your locker. When you do, then outside influences are made powerless.

Let me give you a great example of how these passions can refute external pressure. As I mentioned, one of my passions is my family. It's very important for me to spend time with them. I had an opportunity to take a job that would pay me considerably more money but would require that I travel. Believe me, I am not one of those guys who is going to cry about the evils of money. Money is a wonderful tool. We can do amazing things with money to further the Kingdom of God or do things for our families. But, this was a very easy decision for me. I refuse to make a decision that will negatively impact one of the items on my passions list. So I did not pursue this opportunity and I did without the extra money. I have no problem with that because it's not who I am.

Another example relates to a run camp that I participated in on Saturday mornings during the winter. I turned down all offers if they were scheduled during those Saturday mornings. It may have been something related to work, volunteering, or anything for that matter. I always refused because I was part of a running group that met that morning. My commitment to fitness and this group of people was more important than the other demands on my time. It's easy to turn down such temptations because they are not consistent with who I am.

Now these examples are rather benign, but when you identify your passions and let them help define you, it gives you the ammunition to deal with peer pressure or temptation. They become part of your measuring stick, or cornerstone, or what have you. You know what color you are and you can compare that template to the color of the option before you and see if they match. If they don't, you move on.

Establishing boundaries in your life this way is a very empowering thing. My daughter is in Girls on the Run and they employ this in a slightly different way. Girls on the Run is a program that uses running to teach girls how to define themselves based on their own strengths and not by external peer pressure about body image, or inappropriate conduct or the like. So if someone approaches them with pressure to do something that is inconsistent with how they have learned to define themselves, their response is simply, "I am a Girl on the Run. We don't do that." How cool is that?

You see, once you get far enough down this road of identifying your passions and defining who you are outside of external influences, you are able to see what makes you unique and how that will play into the world around you. If you know who you are, then you are not as susceptible to the demands that are placed on you to try and impress others, or fit in, or be something that is inconsistent with the "you" you have defined.

At this point, we have identified that we have traditionally been prone to deferring our true self to the influence of others for various reasons and to varying degrees. We have taken a step back and tried to make sense of who we are apart from those influences. And we have seen how we can take those things that make us unique and use them to help guide us away from negative influence. Now I want to look at one more area of behavior that, if we can get our arms around it, will sharpen our perspective on being uncivilized. And the question is: Would you rather be popular or significant? ("Dum dum dum duuuuuum." Fade to black ...)

Chapter 3

Fumbling his confidence and wondering why the
world has passed him by
Hoping that he's bid for more than arguments and
failed attempts to fly

We were meant to live for so much more
Have we lost ourselves?
Somewhere we live inside

Meant To Live — Switchfoot[8]

Righteousness is

the New Black

I want to make a deal with you. I have placed two doors in front of you. There is a prize behind both, but you can only pick one door. Door number one is a life filled with status, celebrity, money and popularity. Everyone will know you. You will travel the world and people will shout your name as they see you on the street. You will be on Entertainment Tonight, Oprah, The Late Show and be a guest judge on American Idol. You will be the "it" person. Time will pass and you will pass on and your glory will eventually fade. You won't have made a material contribution to society, but you were an A-list star in your time.

Door number two holds a different sort of life. You will lead a comfortable life with many friends and family who love you. Your kids look up to you and your spouse loves you dearly. You have close friends, the kind of friends that many people never have the opportunity to create. You will make a significant impact on those around you. The world is a better place for having you in it...but, no one outside of your small circle will ever know your name. You will be disregarded by society at large. You never make it to the Tonight Show. In fact, you never make it onto the local morning news show. You are a statistic; however, your life is very significant. Generations of people will be better because of your influence.

Which door do you choose?

Significance vs. Status

Most people do not want to be respected as much as they want to be envied. (Would you rather be very smart or very rich?) We live in a society that wants to be entertained more than it wants to contribute in life. Significance has been replaced by success or status. We no longer try to do things that are significant; we try to do things that will make us appear to be successful or popular. We no longer have heroes, we have celebrities. I don't want to date myself here, but I remember when I was a kid we used to aspire to be like the Lone Ranger, or Spiderman or Han Solo. (My brother preferred Superman and Luke Skywalker but I don't hold that against him.)

These were people who lived beyond themselves. They did not fit in. They served a greater good. They were heroes. Now, people want to be like musicians (I use that term very loosely when I refer to many of the popular "artists" today), or professional athletes, or actors. Most of these people do not serve the greater good beyond being briefly entertaining. Let me give you an example.

Michael Jordan is a phenomenal athlete. He is probably the best basketball player ever to walk this planet. His accomplishments are remarkable and are worthy of acclaim. There are very few people on earth who do not know who he is. He is a cultural icon. Having said that, I will put someone like Winston Churchill up against him any day of the week. Churchill was despised by most. He was voted out of office by a disgruntled public. By many, he was considered arrogant, coarse and rude. But he is also regarded as being the single most influential force behind Britain's victory over Nazi Germany. A time will come when kids won't know who Michael Jordan is. But the world will always be a better place because of the uncivilized life of Winston Churchill. I, for one, am especially grateful because I much prefer shepherd's pie over sauerkraut.

That is what I am talking about here. We need to take this short life that we have and do all that we can to affect eternity and not be concerned with people's opinions of us in the short term. We have so much potential as human beings. We are capable of amazing things. We can be incredibly strong, resourceful, inspiring, and determined. However, most people live a life that never taps into significance in any material way. We are more concerned with being comfortable or making the right impression. Part of being uncivilized is being more concerned about how your attitude and actions will make a long-term positive impact rather than being temporarily perceived as popular. It's about allowing yourself the luxury of disregarding the rat race and concentrating on the bigger picture. Being uncivilized is about being respected as opposed to being envied.

A great example of not pandering to popularity is when Jesus performed the loaves and fishes miracle to feed five thousand people. I have picked up the check for people before and they responded well to it. Can you imagine how popular you would be if you picked up the check for five thousand people? Jesus gave a great teaching and everyone was captivated by Him. He was at a very important point in the popularity hunt. He was coming off a big win and needed to close the deal. So what did He do? He addressed the crowd that was following Him by saying the crowd did not care about miracles or the things of heaven, they just wanted another free meal. Jesus then told the crowd that they have to eat His flesh and drink His blood if they want anything to do with Him. And how did his actions solidify His status of being the envy of those around Him? Well, the oft quoted John 6:66 says "From this time, many of His disciples turned back and no longer followed Him." He was also quoted as referring to the leaders of the synagogue at that time, who would be like the leaders of the church today, as a brood of vipers. Again, not the best way to achieve status in a culture that revolved around the Church.

Jesus was never concerned about appeasing the popular culture. He was not out to become popular. He chose to be uncivilized to be an example of how we can live a life that is regulated by a greater set of principles. He encourages us to not be concerned with what other people think about us. Life is not about being in the "in crowd". It's so hard for us to understand this given the culture in which we live. The information age has made it much easier to achieve celebrity without accomplishing anything. There are millions of people who audition to get on any of the numerous reality shows. I have seen interviews of these potential contestants and they say that they do not care if they win; they just want to be a star. And it works. Contestants from these shows go on to extend their fifteen minutes of fame for years. And the high regard in which they are held is not the result of any form of significant achievement, it's just because they gained some measure of celebrity. How pathetic is it that people who play sports, or pretend to be something that they are not in front of a camera, or can carry a tune make more money than the people who are teaching kids, or saving lives or putting their safety on the line for our sake? This disgusting discrepancy is because we do not value significance as much as we value popularity.

In 2 Chorinthians 4:17–18, the Bible says:

> *For our light and momentary troubles are achieving for us an eternal glory that far outweighs them all. So we fix our eyes not on what is seen but on what is unseen. For what is seen is temporary, but what is unseen is eternal."*

This is a great verse on which to meditate. It's hard to not do what is expected of us by others. It hurts to live a life that is contrary to the standard practice of those around us. The choice to do something that is unpopular is not an easy one. But this verse helps to put that discomfort into perspective. God recognizes that this will be a difficult decision. But the temporary pain pales in comparison to the eternal glory of living a significant life. Pain is temporary, significance is eternal.

For example, I like to lift weights. Strength training is not always fun, but it is always good for me. Certainly, it is much easier for me to sit on the couch with a soda and a Manchester United match on than it is to go do a shoulder workout. But I know that even as my arms burn and are building up lactic acid, I will feel much better for it next week. Nothing worth doing is easy. The people who make the decision to do the uncivilized things and suffer through the hard choices are the ones who truly achieve greatness. This high regard may not be recognized in their time, not that that is their motivation, but it will be recognized.

When I think about the movies I have seen that have had the greatest impact on me, they are movies that highlight people who have made these hard decisions. Movies like Braveheart, Gladiator, Dead Poet Society, 300, or one of my favorites, Spiderman, all speak of a commitment to a greater cause. These are examples of people who lived lives that meant something beyond just themselves. People who were not concerned so much about themselves, as they were the bigger picture, and a fight for righteousness.

I love Spiderman. He has all of these amazing abilities and is saving the world. But he chooses to keep his identity a secret by staying behind that mask. Outside of the costume, he is an insecure person who chooses to remain unpopular and not get the girl because he recognizes the greater good. Putting this in our terms, Peter Parker chooses righteousness.

Quest for Righteousness

In our time, righteousness seems to have been replaced with sincerity. We do not need to be held to a standard as long as we are sincere. But the problem is we can be sincerely wrong. People will be passionate about a cause, or an idea and people will admire them for that, even if the cause or idea is wrong. It's as if passion is the rose colored glasses that make anything OK.

Yes, you should be true to yourself and passionate, but there are different types of passion: righteous and not. Therefore, it's not enough to be passionate. You have to be passionate about a righteous cause, even if that cause is divisive. We have to hold to what we know to be true and plan on there being a price we pay. I believe that we have completely lost touch with this concept, especially in America. We believe that we are entitled to a pain-free life of comfort and pleasantries. This is not true. We need to suffer for the cause. In the Beatitudes that Jesus taught in the Sermon on the Mount, He states that we are blessed when we are persecuted because of righteousness. We are blessed when people insult us, persecute us and falsely say bad things about us because of the relationship we have with God. They did the same thing to Christ. Why should life be any different for us? There are many scriptures that imply that we should expect to be slandered, beaten, ridiculed and killed for the sake of righteousness. It's not going to be an easy, comfortable life. It should not be.

One of my favorite misquoted scriptures is Philippians 4:13, which says " I can do everything through Him who gives me strength." People have bent this verse into all sorts of unnatural positions to justify various prosperity gospels or self-serving interests. They say God will give us the strength to gain whatever we put our hearts to, or do anything we want. If you just bother to take the time to read verse 12, you will quickly see what it is that God will give us the strength to do.

Philippians 4:12

I know what it is to be in need, and I know what it is to have plenty. I have learned the secret of being content in any and every situation, whether well fed or hungry, whether living in plenty or in want.

Here, Paul states that he has had to live through many peaks and valleys in his life. So what verse 13 is saying is that God will give us the strength to endure any hardship, lack or discontentment. Lay it on the line. Let your passion for righteousness bring on what it may. God will give you the strength to make it through whatever is thrown at you when you make His convictions your own.

An uncivilized person defends a righteous cause knowing full well that it will cost him something. You can pick any of a number of pet causes that are in the spotlight today — be it abortion, anything to do with God in school, or any other topic. We can not cower in the face of the pressure that we know we will experience when we take a stand for something. We have to choose righteousness and suffer the consequences.

Let Your Light Shine

The world is a different sort of place today. There was a time when righteousness was considered the standard. That is no longer the case. Part of our call to live an uncivilized life is to be an example to the people around us. We are to encourage others to subscribe to a higher cause and inspire people back to righteousness. In the Sermon on the Mount, Jesus says (Matthew 5:13–16):

> *"You are the salt of the earth. But if the salt loses its saltiness, how can it be made salty again? It is no longer good for anything except to be thrown out and trampled by men.*
>
> *"You are the light of the world. A city on a hill cannot be hidden. Neither do people light a lamp and put it under a bowl. Instead, they put it on its stand, and it gives light to everyone in the house. In the same way, let your light shine before men, that they may see your good deeds and praise your Father in heaven."*

That last part is the key. Let your light shine before men. If all that we do is exactly the same as what everyone else is doing, how can our lives possibly be an example for others? We just blend in that way. Our lives need to be shocking to others. Be different … shockingly different. Do people remark at the way you live your life because your actions do not fit in with what they see going on around them? Let your actions be so refreshing and focused and uncivilized that you are like a light on a stand.

Due to the incredibly harsh economic circumstances we experienced in 2009, the bank for which I worked made the decision to eliminate a large percentage of their work force. I was one of those affected employees. I saw the people around me watch how I handled the situation. I made the decision to behave differently than they would have expected given the circumstances. I did more than I needed to clean up everything with my clients. I wrote personal notes to people. I maintained a positive attitude and never said anything bad about the bank. People were surprised by this behavior because it was not consistent with how they saw others behave. My actions gave me a great platform to explain my faith to some of them and why it was that I was able to take it all in stride.

People all around you are hurting or searching for something. They are watching you. They are looking for something that will help them through the situations that they are in. They will respond to something if they perceive it as a possible solution for them. But we will never be able to offer the solution that we have if no one can see anything different in our actions.

I went golfing on a guy's weekend with my friend Frank and two of his friends. We had a great time and we all got along very well. These were all good guys and I do not intend to imply anything other than that, but they each commented to me throughout the weekend that they were struck by how nice of a person I was. My intention was just to make the right choices and put others' interests before mine — basic Christian stuff. By just doing that, it brought into the conversation my faith. They wanted to know what it was that made me so different, so I was able to share my faith in Christ in a casual manner. If I had shown up preaching to the guys and acting just like them, I would have never been able to effectively share Christ with them. But because my actions were different enough to be striking to them, the opportunity presented itself in a more effective way. I do not know if any real change was made in their lives, but at least there is a thought in their head now that was not before.

David Crowder gives a fantastic example of this idea in his book Praise Habit. He points out that when you see a nun walking down the street in her habit (the black and white uniform they wear), you are immediately struck by her. You are aware of the dedication and commitment that her life represents because of her habit. Likewise, we need the "habits" of our lives to have the same effect on the people around us. When we walk down the street people need to be struck by us in the same way. The way we present ourselves and our actions need to have the same effect as a nun's habit.

The Greater Cause

My brother told me a story about a friend of his who was lamenting that he did not live during World War II. He felt that was a time when life meant something. There was good versus evil. You had something you could rally behind. Your life had significance. He felt like his life lacks a similar sense of purpose. It lacks a greater cause for which to fight. John Eldridge wrote about having a purpose in his book Wild at Heart, which is a fantastic book. He says that men need a battle to fight.

It's part of their wiring. If a man does not have a battle to fight, there will be a part of him that dies. I agree with him, but I don't think that this idea is just a guy thing. I believe that a measure of this is true for everyone. We all need to feel that we are part of something bigger than us, that there is a universal truth or cause to which we subscribe and can commit our lives. The Switchfoot song at the beginning of this chapter implies this. We were meant to live for so much more than status quo.

I remember when Ronald Reagan made his "evil empire" speech in reference to the Soviet Union. He drew tremendous criticism for this speech from many people. Many felt that he should have used a more diplomatic approach and he should not have made waves. But, he gained admiration from many people as well because he vocalized his commitment to a greater cause. This level of truthfulness was perceived as uncivilized by many. But this message was exactly what needed to be delivered at the time. That speech proved to be a pivotal point in the world's perception of the cold war.

So let's do it. Let's make the right choices. Allow significance and righteousness to beat out popularity and status in our decision-making process. Let's risk something for righteousness' sake.

The How

Chapter 4

You come like you promised you would
I want to surrender for good
I know that I need you
And I don't want to keep living life alone

So take my heart
and make it new
make it true
And make it like you
Take my hands
I lift them high
They're yours not mine to do
Do what you will

Ready Now — Desperation Band[9]

I Yam What I Yam

When I was little, I watched the *Popeye the Sailor* cartoons. He was his own man. He had his set of values that kept him in constant battle with his antagonist. Popeye would not tolerate bad behavior for very long. He knew what he stood for, and when circumstances pushed against that, he would step up to the fight. I knew that as soon as he said, "That's all I can stands. I can't stands no more.", the spinach would come out and the fun would begin. And when the battle was over, he would reassert who he was with his song, "I yam what I yam and that's all what I yam. I'm Popeye the sailor man". He was authentic.

Authentic — [adj.] 1. Conforming to fact and therefore worthy of trust, reliance, or belief; 2. Having an undisputed origin; genuine[10]

When I say you should be yourself, I mean that you should be true to who you are without regard to outside influence or pressure. When we allow other people's opinions of us to dictate our actions or behaviors, what we are doing is giving them the authority to define us. We are saying: "I am no more, or no less, than what you say I am." We need to be true to ourselves and allow the confidence that comes from knowing who we are determine our actions. Otherwise, we are no different than a group of teenage girls who all dress the same and talk the same because that is how they get their identity.

Authenticity is a popular marketing tool. You see people hawking authentic furniture, authentic dolls, authentic jerseys, etc. People are quick to point out that what you are beholding is not some imported knockoff, but the real deal. Why should our lives be any different? Why can't we live a life that is not some knockoff of the life that people around us are trying to push on us? We all have true emotion, true passions, and true convictions inside us. We need to let them come to the surface and drown out the noise and static that is trying to interfere with how we live our lives every day.

I am not a big fan of numbered lists, whether they be twelve steps or 21 irrefutable laws. I just don't like the idea that someone simply needs to go through certain motions and everything will be OK. I am a fan of things that inspire a wholesale change to the way people think. I have seen people try to fake their way through something by going through the prescribed steps, which does no one any favors. There are usually short-term changes in that person's life. But once time has distanced them from that list of steps, they go back to the old way of thinking and living. I would prescribe a change that is the result of a shift in perspective or an epiphany that creates conviction. So in spite of my diatribe, I am going to discuss five things to which I want to draw attention. I am not introducing the items as a list of steps to go through, but as a topics that need to be considered as we look at ways to live an authentic life.

1 — Transparency

We need to be transparent people. There should be no veil or facade through which people have to look to see who we are. We are imperfect people. No one has arrived or has it all together. Yet, we do our best to try and imply that we do. We as Christ followers are especially guilty of not accurately disclosing how we are. When we get together, we say things like "I am blessed and highly favored[11]" when in fact there are times when we are frustrated, or thrilled, or angry, or enamored, or depressed, or giddy. We feel like we need to live life right down the middle of the fence — not too upset and not too happy. We are trying to be the Cleavers, or the Bradys, or Huxtables (pick your generation). We imply that things are together all of the time.

It's OK to hurt, or not have things figured out. None of us was born with an instruction manual. We are all doing our best to figure this life out. Of course you are going to make mistakes and be uncertain about things. Everyone else is too. So when we are transparent, others can see the same things that they deal with going on in our lives. Our transparency will draw them to us and we can be used by God to figure out what He would have us do to get through this life. In Proverbs 14:25 the Bible says:

> *A truthful witness saves lives,*
> *but a false witness is deceitful.*

It's amazing to think that we can actually save lives through simply being transparent. But, it's true. There was a time when I was very depressed because a barrage of bad things came down on me all at once. I was really having a hard time with it all. I was doing my best not to let on to anyone how much I was struggling. But keeping up the facade was getting harder and harder as time went on. Finally, I opened up to a good friend of mine regarding how much I was hurting when he asked me "How are you doing?" Once I got it all out, he explained how he had gone through a similar circumstance several years before. We were able to talk and help me work through some of the emotion I was experiencing. The catharsis was fantastic. In that instance, my transparency did not necessarily save my life, but it sure helped me get through a rough situation. Remember, if you have failure in your life, it does not mean you are a failure. You are only a failure when you wallow in it and don't let anyone help you.

2 — Self Realization

Again with Spiderman (I know, just humor me). In the second Spiderman movie, there is a point where Peter Parker is wearing thin. He is being pulled in several directions and is struggling with his identity. There is a lot of pressure on him. So he decides to abandon Spiderman and he throws the Spidy suit in the trash. The pressure lifts somewhat and he experiences a measure of contentment. But the freedom only lasts a short time. Being Spiderman is not just a habit for Peter to break, or something from which he can walk away. Spiderman is not just something Peter does; it's who he is. Peter is Spiderman. After considerable drama, he realizes this and dons the costume again. He is back in his skin and all is right with the world.

Like Peter Parker, we need to see ourselves for who we really are and embrace that person and all that comes with it. We must allow ourselves to be different. The grass is not greener on the other side. And even if the grass were greener, it's just because they are using nasty chemicals or are raking in manure; and who wants to walk around in that? The exercise that we did where we identified our passions serves this very purpose. That process helps us to realize who we are. We are less tempted to mimic others when we have a firm understanding of who we are. I have no idea who said this originally, but I have heard the phrase repeated several times: The you that you are is better by far than the you you are trying to be. Just be you.

3 — Emotion

We need to be authentic on the inside too. Similar to the transparency issue, we need to allow our emotions a measure of freedom. Emotions can add color and dimension to our lives. It's another way for us to become the salt and light that we spoke about earlier. As Christ followers, we can be too sanitized. We have been taught so much about faith and the negative side of emotions that we have become quite proficient at disregarding them and pushing them down. God gave us emotions to help us regulate our lives. Fear does a pretty good job of keeping us out of dangerous situations. Happiness can be infectious and raise everyone up around us. Nervousness will heighten your alertness and help you to be prepared for what may come. As long as we keep things in perspective and measure our emotions against God's direction, we become more authentic people rather than automatons that live a colorless life.

Let your guard down. Loosen your grip on the filter that has been Stepford-izing the you that others witness. Life can be dirty sometimes. Don't be afraid to get some of it under your nails. Laugh openly. Cry hard. Get angry about the right things. Find a hill somewhere and climb it and then scream at the top of your lungs. Let life mess up a little bit of that equilibrium you have established.

In 1997, Jodi Foster starred in the movie Contact. She played the part of a scientist searching for extra terrestrial intelligence. As is often the case in movies, the government steps in to try and shut her down. Then she discovers a signal that is emanating from the Vega star. Among other things that are included in the signal, are plans for a complex machine. So they decide to build it. (No, nothing bad could possibly come from building a machine from an unknown source with an unknown purpose.) As they are building the machine, the plans call for the person inside of it to not be secured. And since we obviously know better than silly aliens, the engineers decide to bolt down a seat for the passenger to sit in. Cutting to the chase … Jodi is the person who ends up being the passenger. (I know. Who saw that coming?) After they start the engines, the seat that is bolted down begins shaking violently. She is holding on for dear life. Then, Jodi sees her locket floating peacefully in front of her. So she unbuckles herself from the bolted-down seat, loosens her grip, and floats peacefully in the pod.

She was trying so hard to hold tight, but her need for control only made things worse. As soon as she unbuckles herself and lets go, there is peace. Our lives can be like that. We hold on too hard and suppress too much. When you learn to let go, you discover that it's OK to live through some peaks and valleys. They don't kill you. You can relax and create some texture in your life.

Emotions are like the side dish. They make the plate look nicer. They fill in the nutritional needs and keep meals from being boring. By having a healthy embrace of emotions, we can add contour and definition to our lives, keep ourselves healthier, and generally keep things from getting dull. Just remember, emotions are the side dish, not the main course. They should not be a primary determinant of our actions.

The key is to experience emotion while we hold to our beliefs, and measure how we feel by the Bible. For example, it's perfectly OK to experience sadness and to cry, to deal with some fear or pain. Use these emotions to figure out what the root of the problem is and address the problem. Figure out how to get our lives in line with the Word of God so that the cause of these emotions is dealt with, then move on. However, it's NOT acceptable to let our emotions control us by using any of a number of excuses that pop psychology draws on to justify behavior that is anything but uncivilized. Remember, we have been redeemed. The appeal that the world sees is when we represent a lifestyle of freedom and peace that they do not experience. Why would you want what I have if I am miserable with it?

4 — Love

Entire books have been written about love. The overriding theme of the Bible is love. I could never do the topic justice in a short amount of time, so I will not attempt to explain love as much as I will try to encourage you to demonstrate it.

An uncivilized person loves as if their life depends on it. Love with all that you have. Love without regard for personal interest. The entire world is out to serve its own purpose. Very few people ever really put others' interests ahead of their own. 1 Peter 4:8 says:

> *Above all, love each other deeply, because love covers a multitude of sins.*

I am talking about a love that overlooks wrong, a love that will cover something that was done to you, a deep convicting love. When you are wronged, people will expect you to lash out. That is what everyone else does. The uncivilized person responds with love. That is a striking response. Love is a powerful response. It says "I know who I am. I know what I believe. And, your actions do nothing to affect this. Therefore, I will choose love as opposed to responding the way you would expect me to, because your actions do not determine my actions." That is uncivilized. That is genuine.

Matthew 5:44–47:

> *But I tell you: Love your enemies and pray for those who persecute you, that you may be sons of your Father in heaven. He causes his sun to rise on the evil and the good, and sends rain on the righteous and the unrighteous. If you love those who love you, what reward will you get? Are not even the tax collectors doing that? And if you greet only your brothers, what are you doing more than others? Do not even pagans do that?*

Let your love be unexpected. Love where others don't. Love is the true mark of a Christ follower. It's how we are to be recognized above all else. Getting angry is easy. Taking offense is the lazy, effortless, path. But to truly love someone requires an incredible amount of work and discipline. It's the difference between being in a motor boat and being in a life raft. You are determining the course of your actions, and by doing that, the course of your life.

5 — Conviction

We need to have a set of core values in our lives that are non-negotiable. There needs to be a line in the sand that we will never cross. The first and most obvious source for these values is the Bible. There is a very specific, very defined set of principles by which we should govern our lives. These principles are God's Word breathed to us. There is nothing else on earth that will provide us with the safeguard we need beyond doing as the Bible directs.

We all know that we are supposed to have these convictions. We know that the Bible is our ultimate source for uncivilized behavior. The question for today then becomes, how are we supposed to follow the teachings laid out in the Bible? It's very common to hear instruction from the pulpit along the lines of: we are human, we need to do our best, God is a loving god and a merciful god and He will understand if we mess up. Although there is truth in this argument, such mediocrity cannot be our perspective if our goal is to be truly different. We need more conviction than that. It would be like a teacher saying, I understand that you do not want to study or read the material. You are just human. Simply do your best and answer what you can. I will pass you anyway.

I Yam What I Yam

Jesus offered clear instruction for us. In Matthew 5:48, Jesus says:

*Be perfect, therefore, as your
heavenly Father is perfect.*

Or God's direction for Abraham in Genesis 17:1:

*I am God Almighty; walk before me
and be blameless.*

On many occasions when Jesus had just healed someone, his instruction was: "Go and sin no more." These comments are pretty clear cut. Jesus never said: do your best. He never encouraged us to give it the old college try or said that He understands that we are only human. He said to be perfect. He said to sin no more.

I know that this perspective is something that people could see as being very harsh and legalistic. So it's important that you understand what I am trying to say. The point I want to make when I talk about conviction is a focus on the intention, not the result.

I am not saying you have to BE perfect, but you do have to hold the conviction to pursue perfection. We know that God's grace will cover any shortfall we will have. And we will fall short — way short. But walk onto the court with the intention of winning. Don't just show up and say that you will try. Everyone has seen a team that is outmanned and they say that they will TRY to win. They don't stand a chance. You can see the resignation in their eyes. Be the team that is outmanned but says today is our day. We are going to win. In the words of the eternally wise Yoda, the Star Wars Jedi knight, "Do not try. Do, or do not. There is no try."

We are so easy on ourselves. We take God's mercy for granted. We will do something that we shouldn't knowing full well that God will forgive us. Yes, God will forgive us, but we need to live our lives with more conviction than that.

There is a section of scripture in the book of Hebrews that I have never heard read on a Sunday morning. In his writings, the author does a good job of establishing the fact that our Savior identifies with us. He was a man, like us. He understands temptation, yet He never sinned. In chapter 10, verses 26–31, the passage reads:

*If we deliberately keep on sinning
after we have received the knowledge*

of the truth, no sacrifice for sins is left, but only a fearful expectation of judgment and of raging fire that will consume the enemies of God. Anyone who rejected the law of Moses died without mercy on the testimony of two or three witnesses. How much more severely do you think a man deserves to be punished who has trampled the Son of God under foot, who has treated as an unholy thing the blood of the covenant that sanctified him, and who has insulted the Spirit of grace? For we know him who said: 'It is mine to avenge; I will repay,' and again 'The Lord will judge his people.' It is a dreadful thing to fall into the hands of the living God.

This passage is very frightening to me. It's sobering, to say the least. What the passage says is if we choose to not stand according to our convictions, according to the teaching of God — if we persist in sin when we know not to — it does the following:

- There is no sacrifice left for us.
- We should expect judgment.
- We are an enemy of God.
- We trample the Son of God under foot.
- We have treated the blood of the covenant as unholy.

This is not exactly a list of items that would lead you to believe that we should just do what we can. We need to strive to be perfect, not in a legalistic sense, but in light of the sacrifice that Jesus made for us and with a sober understanding of who God is.

Hold to this conviction. Let nothing, or no one, force you to compromise. An uncivilized person does not compromise on these core convictions. Remember "It is a dreadful thing to fall into the hands of the living God." Refer back to the words of the song *Ready Now* from the start of this chapter. Let this be your prayer. Seek God to have Him light a fire inside of you to be able to stand firm in your conviction. Lift your hands to Him and let Him know that you are ready. Enough said about that.

I Yam What I Yam

So, the second set of convictions that we have comes from the list of passions that we already made. That helps to define who we are. We make sure that the decisions we make and the actions we take do not compromise anything on this list. So keep that list handy. Remind yourself of what color you are as often as you can. Also, keep the list current. Over time, your passions may shift and other things will take precedence, like if you enter into a relationship with someone or have kids. You may develop a new hobby or establish a new goal in your life, which will affect the items on your list of passions. Then as we talked about when we made this list, let these things be points of conviction for you.

It's a hard thing to stand by these convictions when others do not, or when others are pressuring you to cave in. But again, nothing worth doing is easy.

James 1: 22–25

> *Do not merely listen to the word, and so deceive yourselves. Do what it says. Anyone who listens to the word but does not do what it says is like a man who looks at his face in a mirror and, after looking at himself, goes away and immediately forgets what he looks like. But the man who looks intently into the perfect law that gives freedom, and continues to do this, not forgetting what he has heard, but doing it — he will be blessed in what he does.*

Knowing to do right is not enough. The freedom comes in the doing. Anyone can cave in. Great people are recognized for standing by their convictions in the face of pressure. Do not compromise. Live with passion.

There you have it. Transparency, self realization, emotion, love and conviction. In my opinion, these are several of the more significant issues that need to be addressed if you are working toward being an uncivilized person. People crave authenticity. They rally around genuine people. Authenticity is a refreshing thing. It can be a very striking thing to be in the presence of someone who is true to themselves and gives no heed to the way that the wind is currently blowing.

Chapter 5

The flowers of the field are crying to be heard
The trees of the forest are singing
And all of the mountains with one voice
Are joining the chorus of this world

And I will not be silent
I will not be quiet anymore

Running through the forest
Dive into the lake
Bare feet on beaches white
Standing in the canyon
Painted hills around
The wind against my skin
Every ocean
Every sea
Every river
Every stream
Every mountain
Every tree
Every blade of grass will sing

Make a joyful noise to the Lord All the earth

Make a Joyful Noise – I will not be Silent —
David Crowder Band[42]

Five Tickets to Neverland, Please

I love kids. I have three of my own, and I am captivated by them. In so many ways, they seem to have a greater capacity than adults do. They love in a truly unconditional manner. They are brutally honest. They express unbridled zeal. They have limitless faith. If you tell a child that they can do anything they set their hearts to accomplish, they will believe you. They are completely free: running, jumping, dancing and being in awe of the world God created.

However, there is a point where the world gets to them. It's so painful to watch as a child starts to take in the cynicism and doubts of the world around them. They stop believing in the tooth fairy. They cover their mouths and stifle their laughter. They pay too much attention to the reaction of people around them. I hate that this transformation occurs. Part of me wants to pack up and move to the middle of nowhere in the Northwest Territories where my kids will not have to deal with that influence. I want to take them to Neverland, where they will never have to grow up.

I believe that one of the key attributes of an uncivilized person is that they are able to dig deep and resurrect that child that is somewhere inside of them. Jesus mentioned the idea of becoming like a child again in Matthew 18:3. He said:

> *I tell you the truth, unless you change and become like little children, you will never enter the kingdom of heaven. Therefore, whoever humbles himself like this child is the greatest in the kingdom of heaven.*

In context, Jesus said this in response to the question of who is the greatest in the kingdom of heaven. The greatest will be the people who are like little children. In the same discourse, he goes on to say that if there is anything in your life that is causing you to sin, you should remove it. You should go so far as to cut your hand off or gouge your eye out if they cause you to sin. Do all that you can to avoid sin and be as a child. So what exactly does it mean to be as a child? What are the attributes that we see in children that are to be emulated?

As far as we are concerned in this book, there are three attributes that we have to either amplify or restore in our lives to become more childlike. They are faith, honesty and zeal. If we can demonstrate these three things in our lives, we will be infinitely more effective at accomplishing what God has created us to do. These are three characteristics that are severely blunted, or toned down, in most people. If our lives present faith, honesty and zeal in a stronger manner than that to which people are accustomed, it will draw them to us.

Faith

Kids have limitless faith. They will believe anything that they are told. They truly believe that the red light in the sky on Christmas Eve is Rudolph, that Superman could exist, that their dad is the strongest human on the planet, and that you will always be there to catch them, no matter what. How cool is that? I miss that. I want to believe in things like that. To believe with no doubt or exception. But the problem is that we have been let down too many times. We believe in something only to have it eventually fall apart. We see people pledge themselves to each other and then the marriages end. We put faith in our leaders only to find out that they had sex in the hallway with the intern. We believe in technology, then watch as the space shuttle disintegrates into millions of pieces.

We want to believe, but we have been trained over time and through many disappointments that we can't believe in anything. We are told that nothing is real, that everything is relative, that there is no such thing as truth. So here we sit all staunch, cynical and disappointed. But when we chose to believe in Jesus Christ, God took the roof off.

I heard about a behavioral study that was conducted on fleas where they were all placed in a box with a glass cover. Apparently fleas have a remarkable ability to jump, which I do not necessarily find reassuring. But the fleas would jump and hit the glass cover on the top of the box. Eventually they learned how high they could jump without hurting themselves, and began to only jump that high. Then the glass cover was removed from the box. But the funny thing is, the fleas continued to only jump as high as when the cover was still there.

That is how it is with us. We have a great capacity for faith, but we have been hurt. So we limit ourselves to only believe as much as is safe so we do not get hurt again. But God has taken off the cover for us. We are free to believe fully once again, because now we can believe in someone who will never let us down. But we still unnecessarily limit ourselves. In Hebrews 6, the Bible talks about the certainty of God's promise to us. In verses 18 and 19, it says:

> *... it is impossible for God to lie, we who have fled to take hold of the hope offered to us may be greatly encouraged. We have this hope as an anchor for the soul, firm and secure.*

Also in Numbers 23:19, the Bible says:

> *God is not a man, that he should lie, nor a son of man, that he should change his mind.*

You see, we finally have something in our lives that we can trust implicitly. He will never let us down. He will never fail us. We can believe that things will be accomplished in spite of what we see going on around us. We are not subject to this world as we once were. Faith changes the world. The path that Jesus walked is crowded with people who were healed because of their faith — whose lives were changed because they chose to believe. We can do that, if we stop letting the world dictate us.

For circumstances to continue to dictate our ability to exercise faith would be similar to the way that a trainer will break an elephant. Elephants are huge powerful creatures that can do whatever they want. But a trainer will securely chain one of the elephant's legs, use loud noises, and bright lights to train the elephant to fear the trainer and do as it's told. Once the will of the elephant is broken, they can then use the animal for the intended purpose. They can also keep the animal in place by putting a chain around the elephant's leg but securing it with only a small wooden stake. The elephant could easily pull out the stake and go on its way, but it does not even try because he has learned not to do so.

So here we are, having been redeemed by Christ, and we now can operate under a completely new set of rules. But we choose not to live in that freedom. The world has trained us and scared us into believing that it is more powerful than we are. But it's not true. We are children of the most-high God. If we will just tug on that stake, our chain will come free and we could wreak havoc on the world ... a good liberating happy havoc.

UNCiVILIZED

So how do we restore, or in some cases find, such a faith? To a very large degree, faith is simply making the choice to believe; acting in spite of what you see around you. Like the Bible says in Hebrews 11:1,

> Now faith is being sure of what we hope for and certain of what we do not see.

Even if what we see around us does not seem to be in sync with us, choose to believe. Choose to move forward in what you know to be true and wait for the world to catch up with you. I know that sounds like a copout, but growing your faith really is that simple. If you want to be a better basketball player, you play basketball. If you want to have greater faith, act out in faith.

Another aspect of faith comes from taking the time to know someone. Have you ever done the exercise where you stand with your back to someone and fall backwards to have them (hopefully) catch you? It's easy if you know the person because you have developed faith in them. That is what we need to do. It will be considerably harder for us to live a life of faith in God and His ability if we do not know Him. Romans 10:17 says:

> Consequently, faith comes from hearing the message, and the message is heard through the word of Christ.

How can we believe that God loves us and that He will look out for us and direct our paths if we do not even know Him well enough to get to that place? A great example of needing to be well informed is when my family bought our minivan. (Yes, we became a minivan family with the pending birth of our third daughter. This change was a tremendous opportunity for me to not care what other people think about me. We had recently bought the van and were on our way home from the American Girl Store in Chicago and I stopped for gas. Then a bright red tricked out Hummer with huge tires and a bigger stereo pulled up next to me. Here I am with a Chrysler Town and Country filled with bright red bags of doll clothes and we just sort of nod at each other. He did a good job of not letting his jealousy of my ride show.) We really liked how big the van was and how it was such a perfect vehicle for us, but we were frustrated that there was just this tiny glove compartment. I could haul 4X8 sheets of plywood without batting an eye but I had nowhere to put my gloves (because that is what you put in a glove compartment).

So we drove around for weeks with our gloves sliding willy-nilly all over the floor. When I finally had enough, I went out and bought one of those organization things that sit on the floor between the seats. All was right with the world again, and then it happened. We found the convenient and spacious drawer that the engineers at Chrysler had so graciously put under the passenger seat. The drawer was there the whole time. I just did not read the manual.

In the same way, God has a plan for you that you can put your faith in, but you have to know that God's plan is there. The way that you acquaint yourself with His plan is through getting to know Him. The more that you read the Bible and pray and take the time to get to know God, the easier it will be for you to fall back and trust that He will be there to catch you. That is how we build our faith.

Honesty

Kids are brutally honest. I remember one time when we had spent the weekend with my brother and his family. I had my hair cut while I was up there by the barber that my brother uses. There is a fantastic barbershop there that is very old school. You know the kind where they do not ask you how you want your hair cut, you just sit down then they cut it the way a man's hair is supposed to be cut? They have the combs in the blue tube of disinfectant, the hot lather and straight razor for your neck, everything the way it's supposed to be. So as we were pulling out of the driveway to head home, my daughter Madeline, who was seated behind me, said "Dad, your hair is just like Uncle Scott's". She was only a couple years old at the time, so I was proud that she was so observant. I told her that I went to the same barber that Uncle Scott uses and she said: "No, you both have the same hole in your hair." (Yes, that would be a bald spot.)

I rely heavily on my kids to tell me the truth, even if it hurts. Sometimes, I especially rely on their honesty when it hurts. One aspect of a child-like honesty is that they are very truthful about you. Kids will tell you when you have chocolate on your face, or a spot on your tie, or if you are being mean. They will not mince words or measure their response. They will be honest with you. The pastor of the church I attended when I lived in Colorado Springs had a saying that he always used when he was about to tell you something that was going to be hard to hear. He would start out by saying: "I am about to be the best friend that you ever had." He would then tell you to get your act together. But he spoke the truth to you without regard to how his words would affect your psyche, and the result always served toward your good.

We need to be that honest with people in speaking truth to them. This honesty is only with regard to speaking the truth in people's lives in love, not out of maliciousness. Consider the following example. Let's say I have a friend who is getting overweight and is putting undue pressure on the seams of his pants. The trick is to convey this truth to him in love.

GOOD

Friend:	"You know Chad, I feel like I need to get back on the exercise wagon."
Me:	"That's great. Can I help at all?"
Friend:	"You know me pretty well. Is there an area you think I should concentrate on at first?"
Me:	"Well, if I were you, I would probably concentrate on exercises that target the hips, glutes and upper hamstring area. I just think that that is the area of your physique that could benefit the most from exercise at this point."
Friend:	"Gosh Chad, you are such a great friend. Thanks for your help."
Me	"No problem."

BAD

Friend:	"You know Chad, I can't help but notice that your hairline is really receding."
Me:	"Yeah, well you have a huge butt."
Friend:	"You suck."
Me:	"Whatever."

Do you see the difference?

We cannot be afraid to speak the truth to people. You may be the only person in their life that has ever presented the truth to them. If we have an opportunity to help someone, and we keep our mouth closed because we are afraid of embarrassing ourselves, we do a tremendous disservice to them, to us and to God. God does not provide direct communication via handwriting on the wall too often. That is what we are for. So if we sit idly by and tell someone that everything is going to be OK when they tell you that they are hurting, we are simply deceiving ourselves. Everything may not be OK. Changes may need to occur, and hard decisions may need to be made. In Ephesians 4, the Bible talks about our struggle to get on with others and how we are trying to be more like Christ. Verse 15 says:

> *Instead, speaking the truth in love,*
> *we will in all things grow up into him*
> *who is the Head, that is, Christ.*

We run into people all day long who are being jostled and shaken by the world around them. We have to not be afraid and be honest with them when we are presented with an opportunity to do so. My brother told me a story about a situation on a highway in England where a dense fog had moved in and an accident had occurred. There was a plain-clothed officer who was informed of the accident and he had pulled off the highway a little way before the accident. He was trying to wave cars over to the side of the road or get them to slow down. People just sped past him at highway speed and were crashing into the pile-up, many of whom were dying. He could hear the crashes as the cars sped by him. In tears, he became desperate and began throwing construction barrels into the road to get the cars to stop. Eventually, he was able to get the response he needed from the other drivers, but only after his willingness to look foolish in the process.

We are like that man. There are people all around us who are headed toward pain, frustration or even death. We have to be honest with them and not care what others' perception will be. Just like that officer, we have to be uncivilized and bold in our actions.

I have had many instances in my life where I was blind to some character flaw I had. When friends cared about me enough to be honest with me and point them out to me, then I was able to address the issues and change my life. But if they had said nothing, I would still have those flaws today.

The second way that a child is honest is that they are honest about themselves. When they do not know something, they will just tell you. They are not concerned that you will judge them. If they like something, they tell the whole world. If they love you, they will give the biggest hug and kiss that you could ever want. Likewise, if they do not like something, you will know it as well. They do not try to gloss over any shortcomings. They just lay everything on the line and figure that everyone will just work with them. Such openness is quite refreshing. We need to learn to be this honest with ourselves. We need to be open with people when we are suffering or when we are working through something. How will people be able to help us if we are deceiving them into thinking that everything is all right in our lives?

I am a fan of Billy Joel's music. He wrote a song titled "Honesty" that has some haunting lyrics.

> *I can always find someone to say they sympathize*
> *If I wear my heart out on my sleeve.*
> *But I don't want some pretty face to tell me pretty lies.*
> *All I want is someone to believe.*
>
> *Honesty is such a lonely word.*
> *Everyone is so untrue.*
> *Honesty is hardly ever heard and mostly what I need from you.*[13]

We all crave honesty in others. So logic would hold that others crave honesty from us. It's all about being real — being open with our feelings and our convictions. Children will tell you exactly what they think because they believe it to be true. They will argue their point to the bitter end. We need to be less concerned about how what we say may embarrass us or cause others to think less of us in the short run. Instead, be concerned about how we can live a life with honesty that God has commanded and that will cause us to learn hard lessons and grow closer to Him in the long run.

Zeal

Zeal is the big one. This is the crescendo, the uncivilized battle cry. This is where Luke Skywalker sends the shot into the heart of the Death Star, or the guitar driven chorus after the bridge of the song. If you get nothing else out of this book, get this: RECOVER YOUR ZEAL.

Children have unbridled enthusiasm. They wear everything on their sleeve. They shout when they are happy. They shake and dance when they are thrilled. They cry when they are sad. They cross their arms and glare when they are angry. They sing as if no one was listening. They can be all alone in the back yard with a football and can completely reenact the big play of their favorite game with all of the sweat and tears and the noise of the crowd.

I am convinced that all of that is still in us. Somewhere beneath the propriety and the pain lies unencumbered zeal. That level of energy never left. We have just chosen to filter it, to subdue it. We have pushed zeal down for so long that we don't really hear it any more, but it still talks to us. We need to tune ourselves in to such a level of enthusiasm again. Choose to embrace it. Like a muscle, the more we exercise passion, the stronger it will become.

I love the picture painted by the lyrics of *I Will Not Be Silent* that I quoted at the beginning of this chapter. The words create a great image of completely losing yourself and fully taking in the moment. Allowing yourself to become overwhelmed and giving in to rapture. You are free to do that. You are free to make a fool of yourself. You cannot tell me that people are not drawn to someone who behaves this way. This sort of behavior is wholly contagious. When they see that you are living life on a completely different level than they are, that you are experiencing life in more color and with a better musical score than they are, they will want to know how to get in on that.

There is so much freedom and release and even healing in abandoning yourself to joy, or love, or worship, or enthusiasm, or even pain. Our bodies were designed to experience these things and we should not rob ourselves. Let yourself go. Disregard how odd your reckless abandon may appear. To restate our theme song:

> *I want to live like there's no tomorrow.*
> *I want to dance like no one's around.*
> *I want to sing like nobody's listening,*
> *as I lay my body down.*
> *I want to give like I have plenty.*
> *I want to love like I'm not afraid.*
> *I want to be the man I was meant to be.*
> *I want to be the way I was made.*

More than any other people on earth, you have reason to rejoice. This is the truth even if you don't feel freedom. If nothing seems to be going right and it feels like your life is falling apart faster than you can keep track, you have this:

1 Peter 1:8–9

> *Though you have not seen him, you love him; and even though you do not see him now, you believe in him and are filled with INEXPRESSIBLE AND GLORIOUS JOY, for you are receiving the goal of your faith, the salvation of your souls.*

I added the emphasis there. There are two things to take away from this verse. First of all, we have been saved. Your sins are forgiven, your future is secure, and the God of the Universe loves you. In light of that, how can anything take your joy? The second thing that you will notice is that the verse did not say: filled with a reasonable and socially censured joy. It says that our joy is inexpressible and glorious. You cannot really misinterpret that. That is over the top, pedal to the floor, both barrels blazing joy.

I feel like I could go on for a week on the topic of being passionate and zealous. Find your zeal, tune yourself to it, respond to it and make the rest of the world try to keep up with you. Find yourself where David was when the king danced before the ark in front of everyone. It's a good place to be.

Jon Egan of New Life Church in Colorado Springs wrote a song whose lyrics can serve to prime your pump on unbridled enthusiasm. Say these words over and over until you believe them.

> *I am free to run.*
> *I am free to dance.*
> *I am free to live for you.*
> *I am free.* [14]

Chapter 6

Lemme break it down till I force the issue
You never come around and you know we miss you
Well nobody took your pride away
I said," that's something people say."
Back down the bully to the back of the bus,
Cause its time for them to be scared of us
Till you're yelling how we're living cause you got
the ball
And then you rock on, baby, rock on, you rock on.
On and on.

Wounded — Third Eye Blind[15]

Will You Be My Friend?
[ ] Yes   [ ] No

My brother sent me a CD he made where he compiled a bunch of songs that he thought I would like. He does that a lot actually. I have been introduced to a lot of great stuff by him. This song, *Wounded*, was on one of the CDs he made me. I listened to it several times in the process of going through the CD, and thought it was OK. Then I listened to it one time when it was quiet and I could hear the lyrics. It crushed me. The song is about a group of friends. One of the girls in the group had a boyfriend who abused her. That relationship changed her. She stopped hanging out with them and just sort of sunk away.

Then the friends get together and sound the alarm. They go to her and pull her out of the hole she is in. They bring her back into the fold, remind her of who she really is, and lift her spirit to the point it was before the mess. It is very uplifting and empowering. It speaks volumes of the need for great, committed, friends in our life.

Independence

My dad listened to The Lone Ranger program on the radio when he was little. I watched it on TV. The Lone Ranger was cool. I was always amazed that no matter what the circumstances, and no matter how many bullets were flying around, he could always get the shot off that would knock the weapon out of the bad guy's hand without actually injuring anyone. He always showed up just in time to save the day. And at the end of every episode, much to the lament of the good folks of the town (and a pretty girl in particular), he would ride off into the sunset to seek out the next day's adventure.

Americans are an independent sort of people. We esteem images such as the Lone Ranger, Easy Rider, James Bond or any of a number of characters who do it on their own. When we rely on others or surround ourselves with a group of people to help us, it's perceived as weakness. We harbor this idea that our lives do not need to interact with people. We are on our own path, which is a separate path from others. It's as if we are on different TV networks and the story lines on my network do not interact with the story lines on your network. My life is just a series of programs that I live throughout my life that really have no bearing on other people.

We pay at the pump, use the ATM, get dinner from the drive through, rent movies online and use the self checkout lanes. We can go the entire day without looking another person in the eye. This isn't right. The truth is that we are very dependent on each other and we need to interact with each other. We need to have our story lines cross frequently and consistently with others, so that we can live the life that God designed for us.

It is not beneficial for us to live independent lives. Each of us is one specific piece of the whole. In order for your piece to be of any worth, it has to join up with all of the other pieces to form the whole. The Bible makes this point in Romans 12:3–6 when it talks about the church and how everyone in the body of Christ has different gifts and we are to combine those to accomplish His purpose:

> *For by the grace given me I say to everyone of you: Do not think of yourself more highly than you ought, but rather think of yourself with sober judgement, in accordance with the measure of faith God has given you. Just as each of us has one body with many members, and these members do not all have the same function, so in Christ we who are many form one body, and each member belongs to all the others. We have different gifts, according to the grace given us.*

Getting back to our pointillism metaphor, even if we have discovered our color, we are just this silly dot floating around the canvas all by ourselves when we live independent lives. We need to combine our color with everyone else's to form the painting that God intends.

At the end of the day, one of the only things that really matter in life is relationships — true, meaningful, selfless relationships. Nothing else that we do in life has the potential for eternal significance more than authentic relationships. We could build buildings and they would crumble. We could write books, but they will find their way to a discount rack next to an autobiography of some child TV star. Only relationships affect eternity. When Jesus was asked what is the most important command, He said to love God and love your neighbor. In God's eyes, the only thing on earth that you could ever do that is more important than developing relationships with others in your life is to love God.

When I speak of authentic relationships, I am talking about a relationship where you are free to be who you are. Not every relationship that we have will achieve the same level of intimacy, but every relationship is important and every relationship should find us presenting our true selves to others.

To quote Shrek, people are like onions. As our relationships with others grow, we are able to peel back different layers to show them more of our personality. While it's true that different people will have varying images of us based on how far the onion is pealed, no one's opinion of us will be less than true. This is because each layer is shown for who you are at that level of revelation. Each layer is genuine.

The end goal in being uncivilized should not be about making you a better individual. The goal is about making you more effective to have healthy relationships with other people. God is not about making individuals, He is about building the Church. You need people in your life to assist in God's effort to remove things that would inhibit you from interacting effectively with others.

In our lives, we will have relationships that will fit within three different parameters. These parameters can be defined as: Courteous, Familiar, and Intimate. I am not going to spend much time on the first two. This whole idea of varying circles of friendship has been analyzed enough by others. I want to focus on the types of relationships that will hold us accountable to the person we have defined ourselves to be. We need to have a small group of people who will know us better than any other. They will know what we are about and will make sure that we stay on track.

Courteous Relationships

This group consists of the general public. This is the group of people who really sees the least of who we are. These relationships do not go beyond the surface. They are the polite interactions you have with strangers or people that you see infrequently. You never really get beyond small talk and light-hearted banter with these people, which is fine. There is nothing really invested. There is no risk of getting hurt or misunderstood, because you never get to a point where there is such potential.

Your goal in these relationships is to be that burst of fresh air that strikes them as being uplifting. You have no idea who these people are or what they are going through, so you may be that thirty second glimmer of

71

sunshine that they needed to get through the day. Make the goal of being a brief glimpse of God to them more important than how you may feel at the moment. Consider yourself to be on stage.

Familiar Relationships

These are the people that you know reasonably well. They are people in your social group, at work, at church, your neighbors, etc. You have more invested in these people. Your conversations can cover more significant topics and as such, there is the potential for a falling out. These require a little more work, and reveal more layers of who you are. In our lives there may be hundreds of people who will fit in this category. We can have great relationships with these people that will definitely go beyond the superficial. However, there is still a line that we don't cross with them. We are still guarded and we keep these relationships at a bit of an arm's length.

Your goal with familiar relationships is to be salt and light. They will know you well enough to know that you are a Christ follower. So they are watching you for consistency and hypocrisy. If you are consistent in living an uncivilized life in front of them, over time, you will have an amazing impact on them. You may be the person who has planted the seed in their life that leads them to God. Don't be the person who sours them to Christianity because you were having a bad day.

I have a fantastic example of how this happened in one of the familiar relationships I have in my life. The opportunity came about with a friend of mine whom I have known for over twenty years. While he believes in God, I would not say that he is a Christ follower. In fact, he has had plenty of occasions where Christians would have judged him and criticized him. Because of that, I have made a point of just loving this guy and trying my best to behave as Jesus would with him. Which was easy to do because he is a great guy. I always made a point of letting him know about my faith and my commitment to God, but I have never "preached" to him. Well last month, the subject of Jesus came up in a conversation, so I asked him what he thought about faith and God. He gave me his perspective, which was generally receptive, but inconsistent with the gospel.

Then I made the decision to cross the line with him. I proceeded to point out to him that I have never hidden my faith from him. I have made my commitment to following Christ fairly obvious in conversations and in my behavior around him. He agreed. I also pointed out that in the twenty years that I have known him, I have never shoved God down his throat or judged him. He said that he has always respected me for that and that my lifestyle around him is why he was willing to even talk to me about God.

So I went on to say that if he has seen any truth in my life, or anything that he views as free, loving or liberating, then I wanted him to talk to me. If I had not done my best to consistently be salt and light to this friend, then I would have never had the opportunity to have a meaningful conversation with him. In fact, any inconsistency would have only fed the negative impression that he would have had of Christ followers. Hopefully, it does not take twenty years to develop such an opportunity with someone. But even if it takes fifty years, we need to be consistent with people.

Intimate Relationships

Promise Keepers called them Accountability Groups. Steven Covey called them your circle of influence. I have called them Scott, and Marty, and Pat, and Matthew, and Dan, and Tim, and several other names throughout my life. Whatever you want to call them, these are the people with whom you know you are free to be who you are, flaws and all, without fear of judgment. They are your confidants.

This is a very special relationship. There will be a bond and a connection that very few people ever have. There is a scene in William Shakespeare's *Henry V* where the king is about to take his men into battle. They are severely out manned and morale is low. So Henry steps up and offers a stirring speech that reminds the men of the bond they have and their commitment to each other and the greater cause. That speech includes the following:

We few, we happy few, we band of brothers. For anyone who fights with me today shall be my brother. Be he ne'er so vile, this day shall gentle his condition. And gentlemen in England now a'bed shall call themselves cursed and hold their manhood cheap whilst anyone speaks who fought with me on St. Crispin's day.

Doesn't that rouse something inside of you? There is something instinctual and organic about the need to have such a relationship with others. These are the people with whom we have no secrets. Confidants

UNCiVILIZED

are the richest possible relationship we can have. These qualities will certainly be true of your bond with your spouse, but you need to make sure that you have this type of connection with others in your life as well. While our goal should be to have as many of these relationships by the end of our life as possible, we will probably not achieve this level of intimacy with more than a handful of people at a time. This group of friends will do three major things for you. They will be your sounding board, will hold you accountable, and will support you.

Sounding Board

One of the first rules of preparing for race day of a marathon is to wear nothing new. Everything on your body has to be something that you have broken in. Your shorts, shoes, socks, and shirt need to be something that you have trained in and know that it will get you through the entire 26.2 miles. The time that you test out new products is in your training runs. That is where you discover what is going to work for you. If a pair of socks has a spot that rubs your foot too much, you want to learn that on a training run where working out such details won't cost you anything. Your confidants will be your training run for life issues.

They provide a safe environment to work through:
- Insecurities
- Questions on issues
- Areas where you need to grow personally
- How to deal with difficult situations
- Struggles you have in your faith
- Why you have a Barry Manilow song in your playlist
- And any number of other issues.

They will help you achieve a clear understanding of your position on any given topic so that on race day, you are fully prepared and know exactly what you need to do.

Within these relationships, you test what you believe and why you believe it. You define who you are in greater detail with this group because they will challenge you. You will work through the difficult areas in your life with your confidants, where there is no danger, so that when you are in "public", you have reached a level of resolution that will make you more effective.

Let's say that you tend to shy away from confrontation. You may not have a clear picture of why that is. Your shyness may just be that you are that way by nature. But it may also be that you are simply scared about a bad reaction based on past experiences. These confidants will help you work through such an issue and help you see yourself from a different perspective. If you are doing something for the wrong reason, they can help you recognize that so that you have these issues resolved in a setting where you won't be condemned. You don't want to test your position on the difficult issues in life with people that are not committed to you. You will get hurt that way, but this group has your back. They want to see you succeed.

Accountability

The second thing that your confidants will do for you is call you to the carpet on issues. No one will know you as well as they do. These friends will have the benefit of understanding how you tick and what your motivations are for how you behave. Because of their familiarity with you, your confidants will be a group of people that will help you stay focused and stay on track. They are not looking to knock you down and be hyper-critical. They are holding you accountable from the perspective of one who wants to see you succeed and wants to help you eliminate anything that may be standing in the way of your success. Think Chris Carmichael (Lance Armstrong's trainer).

Imagine that you are running a race on a track. Confidants will do two things for you regarding accountability. First they will keep you in your lane. When they see you drifting too close to one line or the other, they will help straighten you out. They know where you want to go and they will be the ones to provide an outside perspective to you to help you see when your actions are starting to move you away from your goal.

The second thing these intimate relationships will do is to help you get over the hurdles that are coming up. There are areas in your life that need to be addressed. You will not be able to accomplish all that you want with your life until these deficiencies are dealt with. You may not even be able to see them. Confidants will help to point these issues out to you so you can see how certain behaviors will prohibit your success. Then they help you address these behaviors so you are able to run freely.

Accountability is significant. Many areas in our life would be hard to get through alone. Your confidants care deeply about you and want to come along side you and work toward your success. They are not judging you, they are coaching you and holding you responsible to the life that you say you want to live. While accountability is sometimes painful for you, it's always beneficial. Success does not come by default. Failure is the natural default. Success comes with tremendous effort and the submitting of yourself to the help of others who are headed in the same direction as you.

I remember one instance where this accountability was particularly effective for me. I had the propensity to be a selfish and greedy person. This behavior would raise its head at various times in my life, but I was unaware of the extent to which it was affecting me. Thankfully I had a group of people with whom I was very close in this accountability capacity. They were able to put the pieces together by witnessing my behavior over time. They then sat me down one day in my office in Colorado Springs and had an intervention of sorts. They called me out on some behavior that they had observed and pointed out how it was an area of my life that had to be addressed before I would be able to move on toward what God had planned for me.

This confrontation really hurt. I was upset that I had selfishness in my life and that I was blind about how it had consumed me. It also hurt to know that I was letting my friends down. But, we were able to work through my behavior and its causes and get me over that hurdle in my life. Now one of my primary life goals is to be considered by everyone I meet to be one of the more selfless and generous people they know. I could have never gotten to this point without that group of people who stepped up and called me out on that issue.

Your confidants will be your partners. You will commit to being completely truthful with them and they will not condemn you, but speak the truth back to you in love. There are no secrets with them. Because of all that will be accomplished, you will be a better person for having them in your life.

Support

The final thing these friends do is act as a support group. They will be the ones that know how to pray for you regarding the best and worst things about you. They will be the ones to whom you can completely open up.

We all go through difficult times in our lives. At those times, confidants will be the ones that will build us up when we are at our weakest. They will offer a shoulder, counsel, or encouragement. Because they know you better than most, they will be able to help you through tough circumstances more effectively. They will know what you need at that time. They are the ones who are praying for you consistently.

Take Jesus' relationship with Peter for instance. Remember that Peter was one of the "big three". It was always Peter, James and John were there, or Peter, James and John did this. They were consistently shown to have the closest relationship with Jesus. And yet, Peter still failed by denying his association with Jesus. It was in this context that Jesus showed how intimate relationships can provide support for each other. Jesus prayed that Peter's faith would not fail. He prepared Peter for what was coming, prayed for him through the process, and restored and encouraged him afterward. It is because of the intimate relationships you will have with others that you will know exactly what they need and how to support them during periods of trial in their lives.

The Friend Interview

You don't just happen upon an intimate level of a relationship. This level of interaction is very deliberate and proactive. Because of what is at stake in confidant relationships, you need to be particular when you are moving toward them. There are some things that will serve as guidelines for you as you consider potential "candidates". These will help to make sure that you are partnering with like-minded people who are appropriately matched for you. Certainly, you do not want to be surrounded by people who are exactly like you. Otherwise, you will not be able to benefit from a different perspective. But there are some general categories that have to be the same or the fit will be bad and the relationship will not be as effective as it could be. You are looking for people who fit the bill of the St Crispin's Day speech, people who are committed to that to which you are committed.

1. Are you going where I am going?

You know what you want to accomplish in your life. You know the goals you have and the speed and intensity with which you are going to accomplish them. You want people around you who are going to encourage that. I have had several instances in my life where I was working toward this intimate level of a relationship with different people. In the discovery process, I was able to quickly determine that the fit was not going to be right. They were people who were too content with the status quo. I just can't do that. I need people who are pushing as hard as I am to do more and be more. I know that God has amazing things He wants to do in my life and I am straining at the reigns to get there. I need someone who wants to get there in their life as badly as I want to in mine. Similarly, I would have been bad for them. In the end, I would only have stressed them out.

The need for similarity does not mean that you have to be doing the exact same thing, just that you are both wired to run at the same speed. Picture yourself on a cruise ship. You may be a swimming pool and exercise room sort of person and she may be a deck chair and a book sort. You may be accomplishing different things with your life, but you are on the same ship, going the same direction at the same speed. You don't want to develop a covenant sort of relationship with someone on a barge. She will not be able to identify with you and will have a hard time understanding why you are trying to accomplish what you want with your life. Instead of supporting you, she will end up pulling you back.

For example, when I was living in Colorado Springs, I had this sort of relationship with a friend named Matthew. He is one of my best friends in the world, but at the time, our lives were very different. He was a musician, father, home-owner, and from California. I was starting a small non-profit organization, no kids, renting, and from Michigan. There was much that was different about us. But, we were both running as hard and as fast as we could toward the direction of God's call on our lives. Because of that, we connected on many levels and were able to serve each other well in our friendship. So be with people who are going the same speed as you.

2. Are You About What I Am About?

What are your passions? What are the things on which you will not compromise? What are your convictions and the things that inspire you to live the way you do? There needs to be overlap in these areas. You will both have a circle in your life that represents all of these passions and convictions. Your circles will not be identical, but they need to overlap significantly enough to encompass a majority of these items.

There is one item that absolutely has to be consistent between you and your confidants. That is faith. This is a deal-breaker. If they are not passionately living their life in pursuit of all that God has planned for them, then accountability will never work. I have a great friend in my life that will never get to the point of having an accountability sort of relationship with me because he does not have the same relationship with God that I do. He is a great guy. I have tremendous respect for him and really care for him. But I will not let him speak into my life on the deep issues because he is not looking to have God speak through him to me. There has to be a passionate pursuit of God in their life for you to consider moving to this level of friendship with them.

While other areas pale in comparison to the faith issue, they are nonetheless important. Make sure that your confidants are wired the same

way you are. Some of the things that I am about that I need to see in my
friends are:
- Are they looking to live an uncivilized life?
- Are they committed to their marriage and family?
- Are they pursuing fitness?
- Are they about significant relationships with people?
- Do they demonstrate passion in their life?
- Can they have fun and laugh often?
- Will they concede that Manchester United is the greatest team in the EPL?

When you are considering partnering with someone in an
accountability relationship, you want it to be with people who will
encourage you in the things that you want to pursue. If they cannot
identify with you and with your passions, they have no basis to encourage
or support you. How can a friend help me through a rough patch with my
wife, when he is not committed to his marriage to that extent? So surround
yourself with like-minded people. As I mentioned before, there is finesse
here. You do not want to surround yourself with clones. As long as the
major convictions are there, the details can vary. You can even consider
someone who is an Arsenal or Liverpool soccer fan. (Although I do not
recommend doing so.)

3. Are You Committed to this Relationship?

Confidant relationships are not something that you do half-
heartedly. Moving toward this magnitude of connection with someone is a
lot of work and there is a lot at risk. You need to be very upfront and
deliberate with each other when you are considering moving forward.
There needs to be a mutual commitment to accept each other as you are.
There can be no condemnation. You have to be willing to speak truthfully
to each other in love, from the perspective of helping each other through
life. There must be a commitment to confidentiality. You will share very
intimate things and they have to be held in trust. You need to commit to
support each other. You will be praying for each other. You need to be
willing to get that phone call at three in the morning when they are broken
and need help. The commitment level has to be the same for both of you.
You cannot approach someone with only one foot in the water.

Your confidants will help take you to places in your life where you
want to be, but have not been able to go on your own. They are your Band
of Brothers or your Ya Ya Sisterhood. If part of being uncivilized is a
wholesale commitment to authentic relationships, then this level of

relationship is necessary. Your confidants are your friends, coaches, counselors, and test subjects. They will help get you to your destination. You will not have more than a few people in your life who will function in this capacity with you at any given time. Establishing relationships of this sort may sound like a lot of work, or make you uncomfortable and that is because it's supposed to. Going back to our race, if you are not working hard and pushing yourself out of your comfort zone, all you can hope to accomplish with your life is what you are already accomplishing. You need to get a little uncomfortable, maybe even a lot uncomfortable.

The Why

Chapter 7

You're arriving with the sound of the thunder and
rain.
You're arriving in the calm of the wind and the
waves.
You're arriving in the glow of a burning flame, a
burning flame.

Praise awaits You at the dawn when the world
comes alive.
Praise awaits You in the darkness and shines in
the light.
Praise awaits You with a song of love and desire,
love and desire.

Here comes the King.
All bow down.
Lift up your voices unto the Lamb.
He is the King.
All bow down, all bow down.

All Bow Down — Chris Tomlin[16]

Dirty Lips

When I graduated from college, I moved out to Colorado Springs and started a financial counseling ministry. I was working with people who were having a difficult time managing their personal finances. I would help them with issues as simple as learning to balance a checkbook, to as complex as avoiding bankruptcy. But no matter what the issue, I would always try to convey to my clients that "why" they were there was the most important part. People would come in and just want to know how they were going to get out of their specific situation. But if all you do is learn a technique, then the incentive for that technique will eventually wane. But if you know WHY you are doing something, then the technique becomes secondary.

For example, if your house is on fire, you are going to get out of the house. How you do it becomes irrelevant. You may leave through a door, through a window, or just barrel right through the wall. You do not care how, you simply have a solid understanding of why you need to get out. That is how it is in our desire to live an uncivilized life. I could discuss factors such as being an authentic person, having a close group of friends, being childlike, etc., but that would only get you so far. We need to get the holiness of God deeply imbedded in us. Then we have the "why". When we know the reason for the need to change the way we live our lives, then the details become less important.[17]

I have read so many "self help" books, both Christian and secular, that it would make a lesser person nauseous. I know how to make more friends, make more money, be more successful, manage people better, lose weight, gain muscle, influence people, build relationships, and any other improvement that you would choose to make. There are many fantastic things that are said in these books by very intelligent people. But the thing is, after having exposed myself to so much of that, you get to a point where the instruction (and proposed motivation) all just start to run together. You need to have a deeper reason to work toward all of these improvements beyond self-centeredness. The "why".

Let's say that I master all of these issues; I have every highlighted point memorized. Everyone likes me, I am the CEO of the bank, I won the Ironman competition and I can make the best pumpkin pie of anyone in the state. So what? You get to a point where the accomplishment is empty. You do not have anything in you that is motivating you to sustain the effort, and you can really only eat so many pumpkin pies; I mean … come on.

So I want to make sure that this is not just another one of those books that you read and then get fired up momentarily. I have done that, where I finish a book and am inspired to make a wholesale commitment to change. I am on top of the world for a few months then the motivation sort of dissipates. Then, I am left standing there wondering what all of the excitement was about. But since I am sure that no one else has ever found themselves in that very situation, this is probably an exercise for my sole benefit. Nonetheless, here I go.

Here is an example of how discovering the "why" changed my life. I spent years being more concerned with other people's opinion of me rather than God's opinion. I have personally struggled in coming to terms with defining the "why" in my life. The only thing that eventually did the trick was my understanding that I am saved by grace. I was bought with a price and I serve a holy God. God is holy and He demands that I behave in a specific manner. That settled the motivation issue for me. I stopped right there. I did not care about how to stop being tempted by my concern for the opinion of others. I just knew why I was stopping, and that was sufficient. So let's talk about our "why".

Fear God

I really enjoy learning about the English language. It can be so beautiful. The breadth of the vocabulary available to us is amazing. I especially like to continue to study grammar. The problem is that English is an evolving language. We may have a rule of grammar that was steadfast for hundreds of years that falls out of use. Or there have been words that have been spelled a certain way for even longer that slowly change. When the public use of specific grammar or spelling or anything else for that matter becomes widespread enough, then it will eventually become the accepted use.

For example, ending a sentence with a preposition was once entirely taboo but is commonly done now. We used to spell flavor similarly to glamour, but now we have dropped the "u". There is even discussion of making it acceptable to spell through as thru and although as altho. I personally think these changes are all just the result of laziness and ignorance, and I am waging a one man battle against them, albeit an ineffective one. A third thing that happens with a language is that certain words fall out of use. Great words that can be so descriptive, but we just stop using them. A good example is when the angels appeared to the shepherds the night of Jesus' birth. The King James version said that they were sore afraid. We don't use that phrase today, but isn't it great? They were afraid to the extent that they were in physical pain. Using that phrase really gives you a better understanding of their condition.

Another phrase that has lost some of its meaning is to fear someone. The Bible tells us to fear God and not fear man. Our definition of fear is very narrow in that context. When we think of fearing someone, we usually think of being scared of them in that our personal well being is at risk. But when God speaks of fearing someone, he means much more than that. The definition certainly encompasses that sense of being scared, but it also includes respect, reverence, awe, and deference. When you fear someone, you abnegate your will to them on different levels. We take our desires or purposes and change them to be consistent with the person whom we fear.

At some level, we behave contrary to our authentic selves because we fear others. And because we fear them, we act in a way that will placate them. But you can only have one master. Fearing God instead of man can be very hard when we see and hear our peers every day. We can be easily influenced by them because they are tangible. We don't physically see God or audibly hear God every day. It's difficult for us to consistently let His influence be primary in our lives. But we must. We have to ask ourselves at every exchange whom we should fear. Do not fear man, fear God above all and use that as the basis to determine our course of action. But how do we make God more "tangible" to us?

Part of this process is to make sure that we have a right understanding of God. We as a society are guilty of compartmentalizing and rationalizing God to fit our perspective. Our minds have a problem conceiving of God. So we try to define God according to our perspective and our points of reference. In our minds, we have given God human characteristics and imagine Him to consider things from the perspective of the human mind because that is what WE do. We turn God into George Burns, Morgan Freeman or a painting on the ceiling of the Sistine Chapel. When we don't understand how God could think a certain way, or behave a certain way, then we change the way we consider Him until we are comfortable with our understanding of Him again. This seems easier than changing the way we think to try and conceive of an inconceivable God.

Another major culprit in the dumbing down of God in our minds is the irresponsible teaching of certain people from behind the pulpit. They will only talk about what God can do for them, and how He loves them, and only wants the best for them and how He wants them to prosper beyond all else. They present God as a glorified ATM or a benevolent rich uncle. So one can easily see how it is that we have lost the fear of God. In order to move forward at all, we need to get the fear of God back.

God is holy. Does that mean anything to you? Does that sentence make you tremble with reverence and fear? Or is it just another phrase that has grown trite from overuse. They say that familiarity breeds contempt. That is true in many ways. It's certainly true regarding our perspective of God. Although we do not hold God in contempt, we certainly accord to Him a lesser reverence than He warrants. We need to get back to the place where we understand that God is holy. He is "other than". He is set apart. He is infinitely above and beyond all that we can do or even imagine can be done.

I believe that if we can recover this sense of awe, this reverence, this fear, then our striving for an uncivilized life will be infinitely easier. The fear of God is the "why".

All About God

"It's all about you." I am sure that you have heard people say that with no small amount of sarcasm. It's a popular retort around here. Or the more brazen and ever-popular alternative: "It's all about me". But no matter how much we joke or how thick the sarcasm runs, there is still a measure of truth in that. We harbor the notion that we are inherently significant and to a certain extent, people should cater to us in some way or another. Rubbish!

In truth, it's all about God. The way we act, what we say, how we conduct our relationships, and the commandments that we follow all need to be based on the realization that it's ALL about God.

If we can get this fact to sink in, then everything else makes sense. We can live an uncivilized life easily when we understand that God is God. He is not just some muscular bearded man reaching out to touch Adam's finger. Nor is He some Disney-esque well intended (but hopelessly bumbling) father figure that is doing what he can to help us get through life. God is GOD, the creator of the heavens and the earth, the same yesterday, today and tomorrow, having no beginning and no end — God. His glory is our motivation for everything we do. Understanding this primary issue provides us with a perspective that will make those self-help books make a lot more sense. This is because we will see ourselves more clearly and know why we need to change. Such motivation also holds true to the discussion on how to live a life that is uncivilized, unashamed and completely committed to God and his purpose.

Dirty Lips

Only an understanding of God's holiness will make God palpable to us. Then will we be able to "see" Him in the situation where outside pressure is tangibly surrounding us.

There have been a couple of people who were granted the privilege to see heaven while they were still alive. One of those people was John the apostle. While he was in a Roman prison on the island of Patmos as a result of his missionary work, Jesus appeared to him and gave him a vision of heaven and things to come. Now eschatology is about as clear to me as why the Simpsons is being syndicated in Iraq, so I am not going to even try to sort that out. I just want you to see what is going on in heaven right now, while we are living our self-absorbed lives. In this passage John describes his vision of Jesus.

Revelations 19:11–16

> *I saw heaven standing open and there before me was a white horse, whose rider is called Faithful and True. With justice he judges and makes war. His eyes are like blazing fire, and on his head are many crowns. He has a name written on him that no one knows but he himself. He is dressed in a robe dipped in blood and his name is the Word of God. The armies of heaven were following him, riding on white horses and dressed in fine linen, white and clean. Out of his mouth comes a sharp sword with which to strike down the nations. "He will rule them with an iron scepter." He treads the winepress of the fury of the wrath of God Almighty. On his robe and on his thigh he has this name written: KING OF KINGS AND LORD OF LORDS.*

This is the same person who humbled himself and became a man to die for us and to save us. This is Jesus Christ. I am concerned that we have grown too familiar with the Jesus that is represented in our modern culture. Everywhere we look, we see representations of Jesus as a docile, peace-loving, blue-eyed, bearded (and astonishingly caucasian) young man. We constantly hear how Jesus is our friend, he died for us, he loves us, etc.

89

This is all true, but most of the time we stop there. We do not go on to declare that Jesus is the Son of the most-high God. He is the Word of God. He is God made Man. He is seated at the right hand of the Father. He will judge every man. Read that passage again and try to get a sense of the magnificence of Jesus.

In this next passage, John attempts to reveal some of the glory of God. I say attempts because we do not have enough adjectives in the entire English language to come close to doing justice to that task.

Revelations 4:2–11

> *There before me was a throne in heaven with someone sitting on it. And the one who sat there had the appearance of jasper and carnelian. A rainbow resembling an emerald encircled the throne. Surrounding the throne were twenty-four other thrones, and seated on them were twenty-four elders. They were dressed in white and had crowns of gold on their heads. From the throne came flashes of lightning, rumblings and peals of thunder. Before the throne, seven lamps were blazing. These are the seven spirits of God. Also before the throne there was what looked like a sea of glass, clear as crystal.*
>
> *In the center, around the throne were four living creatures, and they were covered with eyes, in front and in back. The first living creature was like a lion, the second was like an ox, the third had a face like a man, the fourth was like a flying eagle. Each of the four living creatures had six wings and was covered with eyes all around, even under his wings. Day and night they never stop saying:*
>
> *"Holy, holy, holy is the Lord God Almighty,*

who was, and is, and is to come."

Whenever the living creatures give glory, honor and thanks to him who sits on the throne and who lives for ever and ever, the twenty-four elders fall down before him who sits on the throne, and worship him who lives for ever and ever. They lay their crowns before the throne and say:

"You are worthy, our Lord and God, to receive glory and honor and power, for you created all things, and by your will they were created and have their being."

Notice first that John was not able to really describe what God looked like. His glory was so amazing and radiant that there was no identifiable form. John describes Him as having the appearance of jasper and carnelian (colored stone and jewel) surrounded by a rainbow resembling an emerald. Lightning and thunder emanated from His throne. And constantly, without it ever ceasing, heaven worships Him. Try to imagine the scene that John paints for us. This never-ending event is going on right now. It will go on like this forever. Worship of God in all of His incomprehensible glory will never end.

Revelations 5:11–14

Then I looked and heard the voice of many angels, numbering thousands upon thousands, and ten thousand times ten thousand. They encircled the throne and the living creatures and the elders. In a loud voice they sang:

"Worthy is the Lamb, who was slain, to receive power and wealth and wisdom and strength and honor and glory and praise!"

*Then I heard every creature in heaven
and on earth and under the earth
and on the sea and all that is in
them, singing:*

*"To him who sits on the throne,
and to the Lamb be praise and honor
and glory and power forever and
ever!"*

This is our God. This is the one to whom we will give account. Whom else could you possibly fear but Him? I am convinced that if we can just absorb even part of the true fear of God, it will change our lives forever.

Isaiah was another person who was afforded a glimpse of heaven, and his vision changed his life. Isaiah was one of the most prominent prophets in the Old Testament. His boldness in declaring the word of the Lord was awe inspiring. The entire fifth chapter of Isaiah is filled with nothing but "woe to" those who do this and "woe to" those who think this way, etc. So here is Isaiah sidling up to God to get the next heavy prophesy to deliver to some unsuspecting city to knock some sense into them, and what happens? God gives him a vision of heaven.

Isaiah 6:1–5

*In the year that King Uzziah died, I
saw the Lord seated on a throne,
high and exalted, and the train of his
robe filled the temple. Above him
were seraphs, each with six wings;
with two wings they covered their
faces, with two they covered their
feet, and with two they were flying.
And they were calling to one another:*

*"Holy, holy, holy is the LORD Almighty;
The whole earth is full of his glory."*

*At the sound of their voices the
doorposts and thresholds shook and
the temple was filled with smoke.*

Dirty Lips

> *"Woe to me!" I cried. "I am ruined for
> I am a man of unclean lips, and I live
> among a people of unclean lips, and
> my eyes have seen the King, the
> LORD Almighty."*

Isaiah sees God and his response is "Woe to me ... I am a man of unclean lips". Isaiah was a man of dirty lips prior to this vision. He just did not realize his condition. So upon seeing exactly how amazing and unfathomably big God is, he is struck with fear and the stark realization of his inadequacy. That is where we need to be. We need to see God in all of his glory (preferably without dying first). We need to see how God is constantly worshiped in heaven. How God's glory radiates from His throne. How Jesus is granted all power and wisdom. We need a sense of how insignificant and worthless we are by comparison. That the only good in us is that which God has given us. That leads us to Job.

Job was a great man. You all know the story. God saw no fault in Job and allowed Satan to test him. Eventually Job loses his way and starts having a bit of a pity party and regretting that he was ever born. He even gets to the point where he questions God. Job had a sense that there was some inherent good in him, some measure of righteousness that he garnered on his own. God took issue with that.

Job 38:1–7

> *Then the LORD answered Job out of
> the storm. He said:
> "Who is this that darkens my counsel
> with words without knowledge?
> Brace your self like a man; I will
> question you, and you shall answer
> me.*
>
> *"Where were you when I laid the
> earth's foundation? Tell me, if you
> understand. Who marked off its
> dimensions? Surely you know! Who
> stretched a measuring line across it?
> On what were its footings set, or who
> laid its cornerstone—while the
> morning stars sang together and all
> the angels shouted for joy?"*

Job 40:9–14

> *"Do you have an arm like God's, and can your voice thunder like his? Then adorn yourself with glory and splendor, and clothe yourself in honor and majesty. Unleash the fury of your wrath, look at every proud man and bring him low, look at every proud man and humble him, crush the wicked where they stand. Bury them all in the dust together; shroud their faces in the grave. Then I myself will admit to you that your own right hand can save you."*

I LOVE this section of the Bible. God's response to Job is one of my favorites. The description goes on for pages elaborating on how amazing God is. How unfathomably large and powerful, and majestic He is. God does not need us. He does not owe us anything. We could never do anything that would obligate Him to us. So for us to consider a relationship with God simply because of what He can do for us is ridiculous. Who has known the mind of the Lord? So when Job is confronted thusly, he says the only thing that we can say.

Job 42:5–6

> *"My ears had heard of you but now my eyes have seen you. Therefore I despise myself and repent in dust and ashes."*

Job's response is exactly like that of Isaiah's. Once they got a sense of God's holiness, they were finally able to see themselves, their lives, and their ambitions from a proper perspective.

God is amazing. Our limited understanding makes it impossible for us to comprehend how big He is. Everything is about Him. He is the reason for our very existence. We walk, talk, breathe, love, interact, laugh and cry all for His glory. Life is not about us at all. It's so frustrating to see Christians proclaim all that God can do for them as a way to share the Gospel instead of just proclaiming that God is GOD. He is amazing. He is full of power and glory. He is love without limit. He is grace and mercy.

It's all about God. The decision about how to pattern our behavior is due to how amazing He is. It has nothing to do with us. We live an uncivilized life because God commands us to do so and He is God.

The way I deal with my kids is a form of this type of justification of behavior. I will tell them to do something that they do not want to do, and they push back. In the end, all I have to say is "You will do this because I told you to and I am your Dad." There is no arguing after that.

So that is the big "Why?" We are to be authentic and honest and everything else that we have been talking about because God has commanded us to, and He is God.

Slave to God

My daughters are all very different. The biggest challenge about parenting is not just knowing how to raise a child, but to have the finesse that is required to raise three daughters in three different ways given their disparate personalities. What worked for one does not work for the others. Meghan, for example, just has to know that I am Dad and I want her to do something. I have never really had to discipline her. If I just look at her sternly, she crumbles.

Now Madeline on the other hand, will test everything. She will question, and push, and debate, and deny and fight. Parenting requires a whole different level of forcefulness with her. My wife just looks at me and laughs. She will say: "You know you can't get mad at her." I will ask her why that is and she replies, "She is you in nine-year-old girl form."

This section is for me and Madeline and anyone else who needs an over-the-top, redundant, in-your-face approach to help understand the "Why?" of governing our behavior by God's direction and having no concern for other's opinion of us. But any of you who are strictly followers, and have never questioned anything in your life, may skip ahead to the next chapter.

Many people accept Jesus as their Savior, but hold off on Him being their Lord. When we become Christ followers, we accept the fact that Christ died for us and we declare Him to be our Lord. He paid a price for us and we are His. We are no longer our own. We are slaves to Christ. We are dead to sin and dead to ourselves. We must put on Christ (Romans) like the Nun's habit we talked about earlier. We must do as He commands. In David Crowder's Collision album, there is a song "forever and ever etc.". In the song he says, "I am finding everything I ever need by giving up everything". The Bible is clear on this issue.

UNCiVILIZED

Mark 8:35

> *For whoever wants to save his life will lose it, but whoever loses his life for me and for the gospel will save it. What good is it for a man to gain the whole world, yet forfeit his soul?*

Ephesians 4:22–24

> *You were taught, with regard to your former way of life, to put off your old self, which is being corrupted by its deceitful desires; to be made new in the attitude of your minds; and to put on the new self, created to be like God in true righteousness and holiness.*

1 Corinthians 6:19–20

> *You are not your own; you were bought at a price. Therefore honor God with your body.*

We do not own ourselves any more. We do not live under our own authority. God has paid a price for us. As Christ followers, we have willingly traded the measly benefits of maintaining our self-serving will for the indescribable benefits that come with a life in Christ.

Therefore, we do not do as we please with our lives; we do what pleases God. We have an obligation and responsibility to do the will of, and obey the commands of, our Lord. Our actions are not purely legalistic because we also have the desire to please Him.

There should be no hesitation or reluctance to do all that God commands. Any issues with pride are settled when we understand that we are owned by God and we are simply doing what our owner is commanding us to do. So when God tells us to dance before Him, we dance without concern for the opinion of others because we are simply doing what we are told to do by our Lord and Master.

When your boss at work tells you to do something that may be unpopular, you do what he says. You are not concerned about your co-workers' opinions because you are doing what you are told to do — what you have to do. Others would have to do the same thing if their boss gave them such an order. That is how it is with God. We dance and shout, we forgive, we love, we share the Gospel and generally live an uncivilized life because that is what our Lord commands us to do.

It's not our luxury to decide whether or not we will obey God, or to decide which commands we will apply to our lives. He owns us. He paid a price for us. He is our King and Lord. He is GOD. If we are willing to abnegate our pride and will to our boss or our parents, how much more so for the God of all?

God is Holy. There are other examples of times where God chose to reveal Himself to others and their response was complete humility and fear. This is the God who owns me. So when He tells me to be uncivilized, I do it. I do not care what others think.

The Challenge

Chapter 8

And I'm so filthy with my sin
I carry pride like a disease
You know I'm stubborn, Lord, and I'm longing to be close
You burn me deeper than I know
And I feel lonely without hope
And I feel desperate without vision
You wrap around me like a winter coat
You come and free me like a bird
And my heart burns for you

Obsession — Martin Smith[18]

Who Moved My Bungee?

I currently live in Kalamazoo, Michigan. We have a rich music culture here. We host many major competitions and events that are on a global scale. Such an environment provides us with the opportunity to witness an inordinate number of amazing artists. I heard a story of when one of these virtuosos came to town. She was doing a series of performances and workshops during her visit. In one of the workshops, she was showing students some specific techniques and demonstrating her skill to them. After the class, one of the students came up to her and said that they could not wait to get to be as good as she was so they would not have to practice any more. The virtuoso laughed and looked at the student and said that the only reason she is as good as she is, is because of the grueling daily practice that she does.

We often do that in our Christian walk. We look at people who evidence Christ-like behavior in their life and wish that we had it all together like that. But what we are not aware of is the daily struggle that goes on behind the scenes that is necessary to produce such a life.

It's just as if we all want to be the Serena Williams we see playing in tennis tournaments on TV. But we do not want to do everything that Serena does when the camera is not on her. We don't see her spend hours at the court hitting, literally, thousands of balls a day, or the strength training and core work. She is as good as she is only because of the daily battle she wages against mediocrity. Serena knows she is in a fight and even the slightest lapse will result in failure.

We have such a battle to fight every day. Left unattended, your behavior will not tend toward the authentic, inspirational or uncivilized. Instead, you will try to match the flow of those around you. Your default is to fit in. That being the case, effort is required to become the person you want to be. We have discussed the proactive effort that you need to identify who you are and move in that direction. But there is also a defensive effort that is required to counter all of the negative influences that are in your life. You must defend against both the bad habits that you have adopted and the external influences that will try to knock you off track.

There will be pressure. People will push back when you challenge them. Satan will attack you when your life begins to reflect the color and brilliance that God intended it to reflect. There is effort that is required that can leave you weary. Be aware of what is coming and be prepared to push back with greater force.

At the end of the day, we have to come to the realization that God has a specific plan for our lives. Between following the instructions of the Bible and discerning specific promptings He is giving us as individuals, there is a path we are to follow. When we do not follow that path, we are in sin. I know that seems like a bit strong, but it's true. The true Christ follower is one who places all of his hope in Christ. He is called to be perfectly humble, such that his personal will is submitted entirely to God. Jesus was our perfect example of humility and shining the color He was made to shine. He only did what he saw the Father do or what he heard the Father say, regardless of the cost. So when we allow external influences to pull us away from such a lifestyle, then we are allowing sin in our lives. And sin is not a passive opponent. So I want to take some time and talk about how the commitment to living an uncivilized life is a commitment that will require daily effort from us.

Move the Bungee

My brother is a pastor and he has a message that he gives about salvation and the struggle with sin that involves a very cool analogy. Imagine that you have a bungee cord tied around your waist. Before you were saved, the other end of that bungee cord was tied to sin. You may have had times in your life where you tried to do good, but the cord would eventually snap you back to sin because you were bound to sin. But when you became a Christ follower, Jesus took the other end of that cord, untied it from sin, and tied it to righteousness. Now, that is your basis. You may still be tempted by sin and move in that direction, but the cord will eventually snap you back to righteousness because you are no longer bound to sin.

I want to shamelessly steal that image from him and apply it to our situation. We have had that cord tied to all of the fallacies to which we have subscribed on a daily basis. Tied to things like the whole stage show that everyone plays and the need to fit in. Let's just call it the game. Now that we know where our cord is currently tied, we can consciously untie the bungee from the game and tie it to the uncivilized life. We have firmly tied that knot, but that does not mean that the bungee cord won't stretch. If we are not diligent in our pursuit of an authentic life, then we will get pulled away from that base. It's a bungee cord, not a chain. That being the case, we need to be prepared when things try to pull us away from our commitment.

Who Moved My Bungee?

Martin Smith from Delirious wrote the lyrics at the beginning of this chapter. Those words really convey the tension between how our heart feels and what our actions are. We are saved. We are committed to an uncivilized life. We know who we want to be, but we still struggle. We struggle with habits, pressures, tensions, and weakness. But we know that in the middle of it all, our heart burns for God. And that is why we don't give up. We use this burning inside of us to strengthen our resolve to not fall back into the game.

Although we are set free from the power of the game, we still have the potential to exhibit the patterns of behavior that are consistent with it. We have been programmed to be primarily conscious of others' opinions of us and we want to impress them. We have developed a habit of insecurity that does not go away once we have made the decision to tie the bungee to an uncivilized life. It's like leaves growing on a tree that has been cut down. They may continue to grow for a while even after they have been cut off from the roots. But that commitment has been made. The roots are cut.

Since we have deliberately and fully committed ourselves to an uncivilized life, we need to confirm what our obligation is.

Romans 8:12–14

> *Therefore, brothers, we have an obligation — but it is not to the sinful nature, to live according to it. For if you live according to the sinful nature, you will die; but if by the Spirit you put to death the misdeeds of the body, you will live, because those who are led by the Spirit of God are sons of God.*

This verse lays out that there are two responsibilities we have. We have an obligation to the Spirit and we have an obligation to put to death certain deeds. Putting the responsibilities in terms of this book, we have the obligation to live an uncivilized life and also an obligation to resist the temptation and influences that would push us back to the way we used to live. And if the way we used to live was anything short of the life that God designed for us, it was sin.

We have covered the obligation to pursue the uncivilized life. That leaves us with the daily obligation to resist conformity. We have an obligation to deal with the pressure every day. The transition is not something that is done once and is over. The process is continual. There are three facets to daily resistance to sin and negative influence.

Really ... It is Daily

First, you need to know that the pressure to return to your old patterns of behavior will never go away. Sin will never give up or even take a day off. We will contend with sin until Christ returns or we die and go to Him. Until then, sin will be in the world. Our potential to sin is there daily. We have to work out Christ's victory over sin every day in our life. The decision has been made, the victory has been won, but the battle against sin not something that will ever end.

It's as if you were in a soccer tournament and you won. In fact, you did not just win, you crushed every opponent ten–nil. No one was even close to you. You have the trophy. But the other teams keep coming up to you and saying that they are the better team. They say that they are the real winners and you are nothing. They continually pester you and taunt you. But there is no more contest. You have won the victory, there is nothing else to prove. You are holding the trophy. All you have to do at this point, is just continue to resist the jeering and taunts and general annoyance of the other teams. They will want to pull you back into the game, but you have already won. The fact that they lost won't stop them though. Sin will never quit. Every day it will take up the temptation anew. So plan on a daily resistance.

Renew your Commitment

The second thing that we have to do is to renew our commitment to this lifestyle on a daily basis. We are pilgrims. We are on a journey. Every day we must state our creed, revisit our list of convictions, read the Bible to remind us of the lifestyle that is prescribed in it, and pray for the ability to discern the specific color of our life. This is about being on the offensive in our effort to be closer to God. Am I molding myself closer toward the shape of Christ today than I was yesterday? My "shape" will not remain the same from one day to the next. I will either move away from the shape of Christ or closer to the shape of Christ every day depending on my activities that day. That being the case, I have to be constantly renewing my mind so that I am transformed. Remember, the default is not toward authenticity. It is toward conformity. Do not be conformed to this world.

Philippians 3:12–14
> *Not that I have already obtained all this, or have already been made perfect, but I press on to take hold of that for which Christ Jesus took hold of me. Brothers, I do not consider myself yet to have taken hold of it. But one thing I do: Forgetting what is behind and straining toward what is ahead, I press on toward the goal to win the prize for which God has called me heavenward in Christ Jesus.*

Really, to say that we want to be uncivilized is to say that we want to live a Godly life. Part of our daily renewal is that the Father continues to prune those who abide in Christ. Pruning will remove the unproductive parts and cause our lives to bear more fruit. He disciplines His sons and daughters. Discipline is not negative, it's positive. We discipline our kids because we love them and want the best for them. We know that certain behavior will prove to be counterproductive, and so we help our kids to recognize this. This refining process is the same with God and us. God puts us under pressure to reveal impurities in our lives. Then as these impurities are revealed, He can refine them. His discipline is to bring us to a point where we more closely resemble Him. But without the pressure and testing, we won't know what our impurities are. So embrace the daily renewal of your commitment to Godliness and don't sweat the pressure that it brings. Renewing your commitment is the exercise that makes you stronger.

You need to write your own personal creed as it pertains to your commitment to live your life the way you were made to live. Let your creed serve as a reminder of the conviction of your commitment. Be clear about the life you are purposing to live and what makes you unique. You are unlike anyone else on earth. When the pressure comes, you can refer back to this creed and have the depth of your conviction restored.

Really ... It is a Battle

The third thing we need to know about our struggle is that it's a battle. Sin will battle us daily. It will not give up. Sin is an enemy to our soul, and will take the offensive if we don't.

Romans 7:23

> *But I see another law at work in the*
> *members of my body, waging war*
> *against the law of my mind and*
> *making me a prisoner of the law of*
> *sin.*

Sin is not just waiving at us from the distance. It's waging war.

1 Peter 2:11

> *Dear friends, I urge you, as aliens*
> *and strangers in this world, to*
> *abstain from sinful desires, which*
> *wage war against your soul.*

Sin will not wait for us to wage an offensive attack, it will come to us and bring the battle to us. Sin hates the will of God and those who do it.

Hebrews 12:4

> *In your struggle against sin, you have*
> *not yet resisted to the point of*
> *shedding your blood.*

Most of us do not know this type of battle. If you recall, Jesus sweat blood in his resistance to sin in the Garden of Gethsemane. In Genesis 4, when God was dealing with Cain after his confrontation with Abel, God said, "But if you do not do what is right, sin is crouching at your door, it desires to have you, but you must master it."

Sin is always there lurking, looking for an opportunity to drag you down. One or the other will happen. Either we master sin, or sin masters us. There is no middle ground. No happy medium. Sin will attempt to mislead us inch by inch. It will not come to try and take a mile from you. It leads you one step at at time, which is why a daily resistance is necessary. Inches matter. Do not give up even an inch. An inch away is still an inch too far from God.

Satan knows that you have made a commitment to living an authentic life. Initially, he is not going to try and cause you to stumble over anything major. If part of your struggle toward being uncivilized is with having someone in your life to help hold you accountable, then he will try and break up the relationship. But he will not do something drastic that would jeopardize the entire relationship at first try. He will start by trying to get you to let some other obligation on your time interfere with one of your scheduled meetings. Or he will try to point out things in the other person that might annoy you. He knows that these small things could eventually snowball into the eventual deterioration of the relationship.

So stand guard. Be prepared for what is to come. Be ready for the battle, the struggle, the exhaustion and all that comes with constant vigilance and resistance. Just know that it's coming.

Going back to Winston Churchill, he knew what this sort of vigilance looked like. There was a speech that he gave to England during World War II. This was before the United States joined in the war and much of Europe had fallen. Hope was not strong and many feared the worst. It was then that Mr. Churchill went before Parliament and gave the following address.

I have, myself, full confidence that if all do their duty, if nothing is neglected, and if the best arrangements are made, as they are being made, we shall prove ourselves once again able to defend our island home, to ride out the storm of war, and to outlive the menace of tyranny, if necessary for years, if necessary alone. At any rate, that is what we are going to try to do. That is the resolve of His Majesty's Government — every man of them. That is the will of Parliament and the nation. The British Empire and the French Republic, linked together in their cause and in their need, will defend to the death their native soil, aiding each other like good comrades to the utmost of their strength. Even though large tracts of Europe and many old and famous States have fallen or may fall into the grip of the Gestapo and all the odious apparatus of Nazi rule, we shall not flag or fail. We shall go on to the end, we shall fight in France, we shall fight on the seas and oceans, we shall fight with growing confidence and growing strength in the air, we shall defend

*our Island, whatever the cost may be,
we shall fight on the beaches, we
shall fight on the landing grounds, we
shall fight in the fields and in the
streets, we shall fight in the hills; we
shall never surrender.*

Get this sort of resolve in your life. Fight. Wherever it is necessary. However long the battle lasts. Do not let anyone or anything deter you from your commitment to being the person that God has called you to be.

Chapter 9

My heart is racing and my knees are weak as I
walk to the edge
I know there is no turning back once my feet
have left the ledge
And in the rush I hear a voice that's telling me
its time to take the leap of faith so here I go

I'm diving in I'm going deep in over my head I want
to be
Caught in the rush lost in the flow in over my
head I want to go
The rivers deep the rivers wide the river's
water is alive
So sink or swim I'm diving in

Dive — Steven Curtis Chapman[19]

Runners, Take Your Mark

OK, here it comes. This is the commencement speech, the pep rally, the call to arms. This is the point where I shamelessly employ emotionalism and cheesy analogies to stir you up and encourage you to go out and incorporate all that we have discussed into your life. I am fully aware that I am doing so. But you need to know that I love these sorts of speeches. They work beautifully on me. So here we go.

There are two enduring thoughts that I want to make sure that you walk away with when you close this book. The first is to choose your side of the fence. You cannot go through life with one leg on each side. Make your choice and commit to it fully. The second is that there is no time to waste. Life will not wait for you.

Put a Sword to It

The first thought that I want to leave you with is that you cannot live your life halfway. You cannot buy in to both the uncivilized life and the life that others around you may be buying into. At some point after putting this book down, you are going to make a decision. You will either think, Chad is a nut case and we should take up a collection to pay for his therapy. Or you will think, I get it, this is what I am going to be about from now on. Whether by design or default, you will make a decision one way or the other.

You have to make your choice, and then cut the ties. Put a sword to whatever may be holding you back. You cannot even flirt with the old life. Did you ever wonder why it was that God commanded the Israelites to kill everyone, the men women and children, when they took over certain cities in the Old Testament? God commanded such extreme measures because you cannot successfully combine Godliness and worldliness. The bad will corrupt the good. Just like a small amount of yeast will cause the entire loaf of bread to rise, subscribing to any part of the game that the world is playing will eventually corrupt you. You know who you are and you know who you are going to be. Stand in that and put a sword to anything that is counter to an uncivilized way of thinking. So if you make the latter decision, which I hope you do on more than one level, then there will be a little housecleaning that you will have to do.

I have three different examples that I want to share with you to help make this point. These are accounts of three people who literally put a sword to things that they knew would be counterproductive to achieving the results that God was purposing for their lives. The first is about how one man finally was able to make the change toward Godliness that he had been hoping for and how he handled the issues that were in place at the time he made the change. The second is about how another man handled the forces that were trying to enact a negative influence during the period of transition. The third is about how we are to handle issues that come against us once we have made the transition and are living our uncivilized life.

Dealing with Pressure at the Point of Decision

There was a time under David where all of Israel feared God and served him as one people but that eventually waned. After Solomon, God's people split into two groups and there was a series of Kings that grew progressively worse and less Godly. Under Ahab, the depravity reached a low point. They took worshipping other gods to an official level and killed God's prophets. But Elijah remained. He was the person God used to set up a clash between God and Ahab.

There is a scene that builds up over time where Elijah informs Ahab that God will withhold the rain until Elijah gives the word. Three years go by and no rain comes and Ahab and his wife Jezebel have made Elijah number one on the most wanted list. And then comes the showdown scene. We pick up the story after the gauntlet has been thrown down. Ahab accuses Elijah as the person causing all of this trouble for Israel, and Elijah throws it back in his face saying that this is all Ahab's doing for forsaking God's commands. Elijah summons everyone to Mount Carmel to settle the issue once and for all.

1 Kings 18:22–40

> Then Elijah said to them, "I am the only one of the LORD's prophets left, but Baal has four hundred and fifty prophets. Get two bulls for us. Let them choose one for themselves, and let them cut it into pieces and put it on the wood but not set fire to it. I will prepare the other bull and put it on the wood but not set fire to it. Then you call on the name of your god, and I will call on the name of the

*LORD. The god who answers by fire—
he is God."*

*Then all the people said, "What you
say is good." Elijah said to the
prophets of Baal, "Choose one of the
bulls and prepare it first, since there
are so many of you. Call on the name
of your god, but do not light the fire."
So they took the bull given them and
prepared it.*

*Then they called on the name of Baal
from morning till noon. "O Baal,
answer us!" they shouted. But there
was no response; no one answered.
And they danced around the altar
they had made.*

*At noon Elijah began to taunt them.
"Shout louder!" he said. "Surely he is
a god! Perhaps he is deep in thought,
or busy, or traveling. Maybe he is
sleeping and must be awakened." So
they shouted louder and slashed
themselves with swords and spears,
as was their custom, until their blood
flowed. Midday passed, and they
continued their frantic prophesying
until the time for the evening
sacrifice. But there was no response,
no one answered, no one paid
attention.*

*Then Elijah said to all the people,
"Come here to me." They came to
him, and he repaired the altar of the
LORD, which was in ruins. Elijah took
twelve stones, one for each of the
tribes descended from Jacob, to
whom the word of the LORD had
come, saying, "Your name shall be
Israel." With the stones he built an*

altar in the name of the LORD, and he dug a trench around it large enough to hold two seahs of seed. He arranged the wood, cut the bull into pieces and laid it on the wood. Then he said to them, "Fill four large jars with water and pour it on the offering and on the wood."

"Do it again," he said, and they did it again.

"Do it a third time," he ordered, and they did it the third time. The water ran down around the altar and even filled the trench.

At the time of sacrifice, the prophet Elijah stepped forward and prayed: "O LORD, God of Abraham, Isaac and Israel, let it be known today that you are God in Israel and that I am your servant and have done all these things at your command. Answer me, O LORD, answer me, so these people will know that you, O LORD, are God, and that you are turning their hearts back again."

Then the fire of the LORD fell and burned up the sacrifice, the wood, the stones and the soil, and also licked up the water in the trench.

When all the people saw this, they fell prostrate and cried, "The LORD — He is God! The LORD — He is God!"

Then Elijah commanded them, "Seize the prophets of Baal. Don't let anyone get away!" They seized them, and Elijah had them brought down to the Kishon Valley and slaughtered there.

116

Did you catch that last part? Elijah had them slaughtered there. All of them.

Israel had been living a life that was comfortable and non-confrontational. They were fitting in and had allowed negative influence and behavior to enter in to their lives and become part of them. Once the decision was made to adopt a life of Godliness and be true to the way God wanted them to live their lives, a purging needed to occur. They had to put a sword to all of the things in their life that they had allowed to creep in.

Elijah did not just prove his point. He did not stop at demonstrating the power of God and usher people back toward an appropriate lifestyle. If you notice in verse 39, the people all had their revelation. They declared the glory of the Lord. But that was not enough. Elijah had to put a sword to all of the negative influence that they had been susceptible to in order to avoid falling back to old habits. He killed all of the prophets of Baal.

That is what we need to do. Once we have made the decision to live an uncivilized life, we have to destroy the things that we have allowed to creep into our patterns of living. Don't just tolerate them or exert dominance over them. Put a sword to them. If I struggle with greed, I need to give things away. If I struggle with allowing physical things to define my worth, I need to get rid of all of my "trophies". If I struggle with selfishness, then I need to spend time praying for others every day. I don't know what you have allowed into your life. Only you do. So you have to choose the appropriate sword to apply to the patterns of behavior that have kept you from being the person you were made to be.

Dealing with Pressure During the Transition

That brings us to the second area of pressure. After you have made the decision and addressed the areas in your life that you initially identified, new things will pop up in your struggle to embrace an uncivilized life. This is still the transition period for you. You will be attacked more and also be more susceptible than you will eventually be after you have established yourself as the person God designed you to be. So you will need to be on your guard to not allow the room you have just cleaned out to be filled back again with the same demons.

After Elijah cleaned house, the people began the process of returning to the Lord. I say it was a process, because even though the prophets were killed, there were still other sources of influence that came up that had to be addressed. Namely, there were the kings of Israel and

Judah that subscribed to the philosophy and practices of Ahab and Jezebel. Some time had passed since the incident on Mount Carmel and there were new kings in town. Ahaziah was king of Judah and Joram was king of Israel. Jezebel was still around and was being, well, she was being Jezebel.

There was a man named Jehu who was a commander of the army of Israel and he feared God. God sent a prophet to Jehu to anoint him as king over Israel. Jehu was to finalize this process of restoring worship of God to the remnant of people who were choosing to live for Him. So the prophet anointed Jehu with oil and told him the word of the Lord he was given. In the eyes of God, Jehu was now king of Israel.

If there were such a transition of power today, you would expect Jehu to call a press conference and announce the change. He would establish a transition committee to help facilitate the transfer of power and the administration from the incumbent party to himself. He would find kind things to say about Joram and Ahaziah. Jehu would hold a prime-time tribute and make a contribution to each of their libraries. Then Joram and Ahaziah would stick around and continue to fester and stew and stir up dissension and go on the talking heads' shows and raise doubt and rally people to their way of thinking until they could stage a new election and regain power.

Thankfully, that is not how it went down. You see, Jehu understood the need to live his life the way that God commands. He understood that we may not be able to see the full picture as God does, and when he gives us specific instruction on how we are to behave, there is good reason. We are to obey knowing that God intends the best for us. And God had instructed Jehu to put a sword to it. That is exactly what Jehu did:

2 Kings 9:16–33

> Then he got into his chariot and rode to Jezreel, because Joram was resting there and Ahaziah king of Judah had gone down to see him.
>
> When the lookout standing on the tower in Jezreel saw Jehu's troops approaching, he called out, "I see some troops coming."
>
> "Get a horseman," Joram ordered.

"Send him to meet them and ask, 'Do you come in peace?' "

The horseman rode off to meet Jehu and said, "This is what the king says: 'Do you come in peace?' "

"What do you have to do with peace?" Jehu replied. "Fall in behind me."

The lookout reported, "The messenger has reached them, but he isn't coming back."

So the king sent out a second horseman. When he came to them he said, "This is what the king says: 'Do you come in peace?' "

Jehu replied, "What do you have to do with peace? Fall in behind me."

The lookout reported, "He has reached them, but he isn't coming back either. The driving is like that of Jehu son of Nimshi—he drives like a madman."

"Hitch up my chariot," Joram ordered. And when it was hitched up, Joram king of Israel and Ahaziah king of Judah rode out, each in his own chariot, to meet Jehu. They met him at the plot of ground that had belonged to Naboth the Jezreelite. When Joram saw Jehu he asked, "Have you come in peace, Jehu?"

"How can there be peace," Jehu replied, "as long as all the idolatry and witchcraft of your mother Jezebel abound?"

Joram turned about and fled, calling out to Ahaziah, "Treachery, Ahaziah!"

Then Jehu drew his bow and shot Joram between the shoulders. The arrow pierced his heart and he slumped down in his chariot. Jehu said to Bidkar, his chariot officer, "Pick him up and throw him on the field that belonged to Naboth the Jezreelite. Remember how you and I were riding together in chariots behind Ahab his father when the LORD made this prophecy about him: 'Yesterday I saw the blood of Naboth and the blood of his sons, declares the LORD, and I will surely make you pay for it on this plot of ground, declares the LORD.' Now then, pick him up and throw him on that plot, in accordance with the word of the LORD."

When Ahaziah king of Judah saw what had happened, he fled up the road to Beth Haggan. Jehu chased him, shouting, "Kill him too!" They wounded him in his chariot on the way up to Gur near Ibleam, but he escaped to Megiddo and died there. His servants took him by chariot to Jerusalem and buried him with his fathers in his tomb in the City of David. (In the eleventh year of Joram son of Ahab, Ahaziah had become king of Judah.)

Then Jehu went to Jezreel. When Jezebel heard about it, she painted her eyes, arranged her hair and looked out of a window. As Jehu entered the gate, she asked, "Have you come in peace, Zimri, you murderer of your master?"

He looked up at the window and called out, "Who is on my side? Who?" Two or three eunuchs looked down at him. "Throw her down!" Jehu said. So they threw her down, and some of her blood spattered the wall and the horses as they trampled her underfoot.

God told Jehu to put a sword to the remaining influence, so he did. He did not wait, or think about it, or consult with others. He got on his chariot and went to Jezreel and chased down and killed Joram and Ahaziah. Then he went straight to Jezebel and killed her. Not only did Jezebel die, but her body was eaten by dogs so that there would not be a grave for people to reference. No sign of her having been in control.

I especially love the part where Joram and Ahaziah saw Jehu approaching and sent messengers out to him. Their response is a perfect analogy of how temptation will endeavor to negotiate with us. It will attempt to reason with us and calm us down. But Jehu's response was perfect. He called them out in their lie. They approached him talking of peace and Jehu simply put them in their place. He knew there was no peace to be negotiated. The confrontation was over with his simple command: "Get behind me."

You see, this process will not be without effort. Even after you have addressed the issues in your life that you initially identified, there will be new things that will creep in to drag you back down, or things to which you may have been blind initially. One who is committed to authentically being the person God made them to be is a dangerous person. Satan does not want to allow that process to occur. Plan on there being interference. So plan on keeping your sword with you. Don't toy with unhealthy influences. Don't tell yourself that you are strong enough now. Don't even tolerate temptation's existence. When you see something creep into your life, destroy it firmly and severely. Resisting sin is not a game or a test of wills.

It is better to be the person who acknowledges that he may not have the fortitude to battle temptation and so he destroys sin's sources at every chance, than to be that person who is strong enough most of the time but falls because he feels he can withstand the temptation on his own strength.

Dealing with Pressure After You Have been Established

The third example I have is comparatively easier than the other two. Here, we are putting a sword to the things that creep up after you have become established in your commitment to being uncivilized. You know the game at this point. You have made it through the hardest part of making the commitment and surviving the transition period. You are good at making the right choices and know who you are. But every once in a while, something will try to draw you back just to test you and see that your commitment still stands.

You should be able to easily identify these when they show up. You still need to deal with them severely. Just because you are in a good place, does not mean that you do not have the capacity to fall back.

David provides the example of putting a sword to this type of temptation. You all know the story of David and Goliath, so I will not go over all of the details. I will just say that David knew who he was in God. He knew the type of person God made him to be and he was true to that behavior. He did not care at all about other people's opinion of him.

So when he heard that Goliath was threatening Israel, the course of action was clear. David knew the color that God had made him and he lived that color out loud. He went out, and killed Goliath with a sling and a stone. Goliath was dead, God was victorious and that could have been enough. But David did not stop there.

1 Samuel 17:50–51

> *So David triumphed over the Philistine with a sling and a stone; without a sword in his hand he struck down the Philistine and killed him.*
>
> *David ran and stood over him. He took hold of the Philistine's sword and drew it from the scabbard. After he killed him, he cut off his head with the sword.*

He ran (not walked) over to Goliath's body, took the giant's sword, and cut off Goliath's head. He not only addressed the issue, but he put a sword to it in such a way that the affront could never come back.[20]

Let this type of conviction and commitment be your attitude. The strong, victorious, able, and authentic person is not the one who successfully stands in the face of temptation and is able to resist, but the one who identifies temptation and eliminates it so that he does not have to fight.

Carpe Diem

Now for the second thought I want to leave you with. Life is short.

In 1989, Robin Williams starred in the movie Dead Poets Society in which he plays the part of John Keating, an english teacher. He definitely fit into our definition of uncivilized. I remember walking around in a daze for a few days after seeing the movie for the first time. The message affected me that much. In the movie, there was one scene to which I want to draw your attention. This scene is where Keating is meeting his class for the first time. He walks out of the classroom and the students follow him into the hallway where the trophy cases are held with pictures of students that have gone before them. We join them just as Keating has asked one of the students to read a passage from his book.

PITTS: "Gather ye rosebuds while ye may, old time is still a flying, and this same flower that smiles today, tomorrow will be dying."

KEATING: Thank you Mr. Pitts. "Gather ye rosebuds while ye may." The Latin term for that sentiment is Carpe Diem. Now who knows what that means?

MEEKS: Carpe Diem. That's "seize the day."

KEATING: Very good, Mr.–

MEEKS: Meeks.

KEATING: Meeks. Another unusual name. Seize the day. Gather ye rosebuds while ye may. Why does the writer use these lines?

CHARLIE: Because he's in a hurry.

KEATING: No, ding! (Keating slams his hand down on an imaginary buzzer.)
Thank you for playing anyway. Because we are food for worms lads. Because, believe it or not, each and every one of us in this room is one day going to stop breathing, turn cold, and die.

Now I would like you to step forward over here and peruse some of the faces from the past. You've walked past them many times. I don't think you've really looked at them.

They're not that different from you, are they? Same haircuts. Full of hormones, just like you. Invincible, just like you feel. The world is their oyster. They believe they're destined for great things, just like many of you. Their eyes are full of hope, just like you. Did they wait until it was too late to make from their lives even one iota of what they were capable? Because you see gentlemen, these boys are now fertilizing daffodils. But if you listen real close, you can hear them whisper their legacy to you. Go on, lean in.

(whispering in a gruff voice)
Carpe.

Hear it?

(whispering again)
Carpe. Carpe Diem. Seize the day
boys, make your lives extraordinary.

Make your lives extraordinary … EXTRAordinary. It really is up to you. Make your life more than what you see going on around you. Ordinary people pass through life every day unheralded. Anyone can be ordinary. Nothing is required of it. Just throw a boat in the water and sit back and go where the currents take you. That is exactly what most Christians do. But I truly believe that is changing. I believe that there is a reason for books like this being written now. God has more in mind for us at this point in history. He wants extra from us, and we are ready to give it to him. Don't fit in. Don't make the easy choices or take the well-traveled road. Make your life extraordinary.

This is the only shot we get. There is no reset button or second take. If you waste your life being too concerned about fitting in or not making waves, then you are done. If all we do is go after the low-hanging fruit, we've blown it. There are no second chances. We are not supposed to take it easy, or take anything for granted. My mom has a sign that hangs in her kitchen that is one of the better instructions on living life that I have ever seen. It reads:

"Life should NOT be a journey to the grave with the intention of arriving safely in an attractive and well preserved body. But rather to skid in sideways, chocolate in one hand, wine in the other, body thoroughly used up, totally worn out and screaming "WOO-HOO what a ride!"

So as Mr. Chapman so enthusiastically encourages us at the beginning of this chapter, dive in. Go deep. Get swept away. This is it. When you close this book, life begins for you. You cannot continue down the same path as if you do not know better anymore. You know what life demands of you now, and you know that you have it in you to give.

So go on. Don't concern yourself with other peoples' opinion of you. Discover what color you are and paint it all over town. Put this book down, get your sword out and live the life God intends for you.

Be uncivilized.

Selected Bibliography and Curious Observations

[1] The Way I Was Made, Ed Cash, Jesse Reeves and Chris Tomlin ©2004 worshiptogether.com Songs / sixsteps Music

[2] Monty Python's Flying Circus was a hilarious comedy program that ran on the BBC in the 1970's. It was filled with wonderfully irreverent characters. Try walking into a pub some time and shouting, "What is this, the Spanish Inquisition?", and see what happens.

[3] A Pain That I'm Used To, Martin L. Gore ©2005 EMI Music Publishing Ltd. administered by EMI Blackwood Music Inc., BMI

[4] I only used that phrase because it sounds so much like really obnoxious new age psychology that my brother hates and he is going to read this.

[5] No Place for Truth, or, Whatever Happened to Evangelical Theology? David F. Wells, 1993, Wm. B. Eerdmans Publishing Co., Page 61

[6] Saving Childhood, Protecting our children from the national assault on innocence. Michael Medved, Dianne Medved, 1999, Harper Collins Publishers.

[7] I love David Crowder (of The David Crowder Band). Or at least I am sure that I would if I ever met him. He is probably my favorite songwriter/artist. It's uncanny how the words that he writes seem to speak so clearly about where I am in life. He knows me pretty well for someone who has never met me. I highly encourage you to go out and buy his latest album, or two, or three.

[8] Meant to Live, Jonathan Foreman and Tim Foreman, ©2003 Sony Music Entertainment

[9] Ready Now, Jared G. Anderson, ©2006 Vertical Music Songs/ASCAP

[10] American Heritage Dictionary, Second College Edition, Houghton Mifflin

[11] As opposed to olive oil, which is pressed and highly flavored.

[12] Make a Joyful Noise – I Will Not Be Silent, David Crowder ©1998 Inot Music

[13] Honesty, Billy Joel ©1979 Columbia Records

[14] I am Free, Jon Egan ©2004 Vertical Worship Songs/ASCAP

[15] Wounded, Stephan Jenkins and Kevin Cadogan ©1999 Electra Records

[16] All Bow Down, Ed Cash and Chris Tomlin © worshiptogether.com Songs / sixsteps Music

[17] My sister-in-law, Erin, shared an interesting comment about this to me. She said that the people who know how will always work for the people who know why.

[18] Obsession, Martin Smith ©1995 Curious Music UK/PRS/Admin. by EMI Christian Music Publishing

[19] Dive, Steven Curtis Chapman ©1999 Sparrow Song/Peach Hill Songs/BMI/Admin by EMI Christian Music Publishing

[20] Requisite disclaimer: In no way am I encouraging you to put your sword to PEOPLE, as much as we may want to at times. I am encouraging you to put your theoretical sword to circumstances, habits and temptations that are prohibitive to your success.